HOW TO WIN
A WAR

BUSINESS LESSONS FROM THE SECOND WORLD WAR

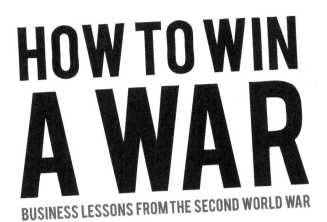

HOW TO WIN A WAR

BUSINESS LESSONS FROM THE SECOND WORLD WAR

Ignacio González-Posada

LONDON   NEW YORK
MADRID   BARCELONA
MEXICO CITY   MONTERREY
BOGOTÁ   BUENOS AIRES

Published by
LID Publishing Ltd.
6-8 Underwood Street
London N1 7JQ (United Kingdom)
Ph. +44 (0)20 7831 8883
info@lidpublishing.com
LIDPUBLISHING.COM

A member of BPR

businesspublishersroundtable.com

Printed in Great Britain by TJ International Ltd.

ISBN: 978-1-907794-15-5
Collection editor: Jeanne Bracken
Translation: Don Topley
Cover design: LID Publishing Ltd.
Typesetting: SyS Alberquilla S.L.

First edition: February 2013

For Paula, my parents, and all those who
showed me the way to Ithaca.

"Those who are only wise after the event
should hold their peace."
Winston Churchill (1874-1965),
Prime Minister of Great Britain

"In war only what is simple can suceed."
Paul Von Hindenburg (1847-1934),
German Marshall

Contents

Foreword

How to Win a War often made my mind drift as I was reading.

As Ignacio was comparing strategies, leaders, and soldiers from World War II with today's corporate world, my mind instinctively conjured up parallel events from my past business experience, the current situations in my professional career, and the contemporary moves being taken by large, public companies navigating markets in full view of the media and their shareholder statements every day. My mind drifted not from boredom or distraction, but from fascination with the book's direct links and application in my professional life.

Allowing our minds to draw a parallel between the dead soldier and the furloughed worker may seem a bit inhumane. However, it is comforting to know that for a large portion of today's global society our competitive spirit these days can be exercised in the office or the boardroom rather than on the battlefield or in the bunker. Nevertheless, those of us who toil daily in suits and ties as well as skirts and blouses have much to learn from the successes and failures of those who have risked more than a career while facing their adversaries in camouflage and uniforms.

Ignacio challenges his readers to assume the roles of General, Admiral, and Commander-in-Chief on both sides of the last great global conflict, and asks "what would you do" faced with the given circumstances. His deep insight into the war on all fronts and its leaders, as well as his personal experiences in business around the world, have allowed him to deconstruct the events, leadership styles, cultural differences, and ultimately the causes that were decisive in tipping the scale in favor of the Allies rather than the Axis powers.

Should you listen to your customer service department when making strategic decisions? What can the battlefield teach us about entering a market slow, but fully prepared versus fast, and unprepared? How does our view and understanding of our competitors affect our success even before we've entered a market? The answers that World War II has provided to these questions might surprise and they will surely lift you up out of the trees so you can look down at the forest. Just be prepared to let your mind drift every now and then. That way you'll be more prepared for the battle at 8am the next morning.

Jeremy Usher
Vice President
Europe, Middle East, & Africa
Earth Networks, Inc.

Introduction

What can the Second World War teach us? Is it possible to see Hitler as an efficient manager? What would a business colleague have to say about Churchill's management style? Did US President Roosevelt take notice of the suggestions made by his marketing department?

This book is a history of the Second World War seen from a completely different point of view – that of the businessman. Because between 1939 and 1945 other kinds of managers were facing their challenges – an unprecedented crisis, a struggle for world markets, new technologies being used for the first time on a mass scale etc.

What was going through the leaders' minds when they took decisions which led to thousands of deaths and unimaginable suffering? How did they react when faced with such unbearable stress? What were their thoughts? How were decisions taken? Were these exceptional men, or just nonentities overtaken by circumstances which were simply too much for them?

Working for a company can be seen as a kind of continuous review of past experiences, especially for those of us who are passionate about History. At the very least, there are so many similarities that it's surprising that that the library shelves aren't packed with books like this.

History is an inexhaustible source of examples applicable to the business world. This book is a history of the Second World War, but it is also about business management and contains lessons which I hope will be of use for everybody who works in a hierarchically structured organisation. Welcome to a journey through time which will reveal itself to be as up-to-date as this morning's newspaper.

1

From the Bombing of Warsaw to the London Blitz

1. Unfortunate Poland

On the 1st of September 1939, at 4.45 am, Hitler invaded Poland. World War Two had begun. For the Polish commanders this was no surprise attack. Their General Staff had known for months that Germany was getting ready to invade them.

They were also perfectly well aware that Germany was much stronger than them, but they felt that their situation was not entirely hopeless, because they could rely on the support of two important partners, the British Empire and the French Republic. In 1939 both were global powers with vast colonial empires. In the wake of World War One they had taken on the responsibility to act as guarantors of the world order emerging from that conflict.

In short, all the Poles had to do was resist the German onslaught until France and Great Britain were in a position to attack Germany from the West.

Two strategies could be adopted in the defence of Poland. Strategy number one left the armies in a delicate position: they could be easily encircled, as it involved defending a 1,120 mile border, in an effort to protect industry, communications and large centres of population.

Strategy number two focussed on resistance along the major river valleys (the Vistula, the San and the Bug), fortifying these zones while awaiting the support of the British and French. The downside of this defensive action was that the Poles would lose the greater part of their industrial zones and some large population centres, while the plus was that it would mean they could continue to fight for a somewhat longer period of time.[1]

The Poles decided to attempt to defend the entirety of the national territory – the first strategy. And just like a nation-wide company striving to retain its position while yielding nothing when faced with the appearance of a huge multinational, Poland found itself staring at disaster. We all know that when, as in this case, reality is ignored so that prejudices can be given free rein, the result is usually a shambles (map 1.1).

**Map 1.1 Invasion of Poland (1939):
German attack and Polish options.**

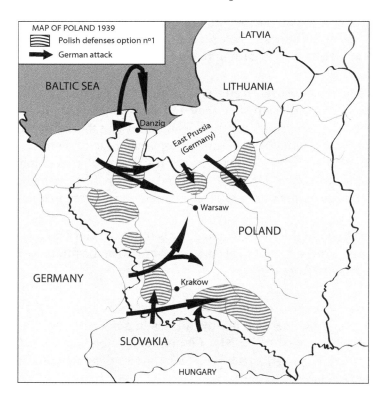

16

MAP OF POLAND 1939
Alternative option
Polish Defensive Strategy

BALTIC SEA

LATVIA

LITHUANIA

Danzig

East Prussia
(Germany)

Warsaw

POLAND

GERMANY

Krakow

SLOVAKIA

HUNGARY

Nor was the attitude adopted by the partners, France and Great Britain, of much help to the Poles in deciding on the right strategy. The governments of both powers gave the Polish High Command a false sense of security, claiming a response capacity based more on theoretical estimates than an accurate assessment of the situation.

In reality, their entry into the conflict was very half-hearted – they were in no hurry to open hostilities, revolted by the idea of having to accept casualties and being forced to take the initiative. The result of this lack of commitment was that mobilisation was slow, leaving unfortunate Poland in a very difficult position, with the partners thinking that perhaps Hitler would have second thoughts and withdraw before they were obliged to suffer losses.

The outcome was that while the German tanks were racing through Poland at speeds unknown until then, the situation on the border between France and Germany, while tense, was quite peaceful with no sign of hostilities between two nations between which war had just broken out. Civilian workers went about their duties as though nothing had happened.[2]

The course of history might have been very different if the Allies had been much quicker to respond, as the book *Decisive Battles* maintains: "Things could have been different if the French front line had launched attacks on the Rhine and the Ruhr (the German industrial zone near the French border). This was all the more certain during the first ten days of the Polish campaign, when at any given moment around 35 German divisions were faced by 110 French divisions."[3]

There's a valuable lesson to be learned from this for our day-to-day management problems. When we adopt a decision, we must be certain that we are going to be able to implement it to the maximum. If we fail to do so, we not only leave our partners in the lurch (our Polish allies: other departments, our customers, our staff, etc.), but we also leave ourselves open to disaster, as, indeed, was to be the case with France and Great Britain.

The rest is history. The Germans overwhelmed and trapped the Poles in three weeks, while the French were still moving troops up to their borders. Poland was finally stabbed in the back when the Russians invaded on September 17th. Where did the Russians spring from? It turned out that they had made a secret deal with the Germans to share Poland between them, so as not to cause any problems. Even so, it still never occurred to France or Great Britain to declare war on the Russians for having invaded Poland. They had enough on their plate with the Germans.

Warsaw fell on October the 3rd and the Russians and Germans divided the country for the fifth time in History (there was to be a sixth, in 1945, when once the war was over it would be Russians who would carve up the country just as they liked).

But why did Germany invade Poland in the first place? Many historians maintain that the Second World War had really begun 21 years before, at the end of the First World War (November the 11th, 1918). Germany had been dismembered and humiliated, Japan encouraged, Russia offended and the heart of Europe turned into a morass of ethnic tensions which would eventually be revealed as nothing more than one huge time bomb.

The 1929 crash brought a somewhat bizarre individual to power in 1933 by the name of Adolf Hitler. Under his leadership Germany embarked on a policy of rearmament and expansion whereby she began to take over German-speaking territories outside her own borders, in Austria and Czechoslovakia. France and Great Britain tolerated these occupations for a variety of reasons, but invading Poland was going too far, and despite that fact that Poland, too, had a large German-speaking population, a line had been drawn in the sand: crossing the Polish frontier would mean war. As we have seen, Germany picked up the gauntlet. Before long nearly all of the states would be at war.

2 The *Führer*'s First European Tour: Copenhagen-Oslo-The Hague-Brussels-Paris (1940)

With the Eastern Front settled, the Germans decided to remain on the offensive, and turned their attention to the Franco-British alliance. Hitler was keen to launch himself against the Western Powers as quickly as possible, but he made sure of the Northern flank first, and overran Denmark and Norway in order to be better prepared for the next throw of the dice: France.

The dilemma facing the German High Command at that time is exactly the same as that to be tackled by a company Board of Directors – who should we listen to, the experts or the innovators?

Experts are specialists in what they do all the time, professionals in their areas of expertise, using thought-processes hammered out through the length of their careers ("we must do the same thing, but do it better", "must do the same thing, but do it cheaper"). Their solutions are usually better solutions to old problems.

Innovators are also usually professionals with wide experience, but they offer new solutions to old problems ("we can also meet the same challenge but by doing something different"). Experts tend to damn their solutions as risky, even though their very novelty often hides much more certain solutions.

Experts usually fail when their ideas do not work because the environment has changed and can no longer be dealt with using traditional thinking.

The cases are legion: top executives of huge multinationals who fail spectacularly when they try to launch their own entrepreneurial initiatives, or, even worse, failed product launches by companies with huge financial and human resources (the Harvard Business Review estimates the product launch failure rate at 90%).

In 1940 the German High Command proposed the Yellow Plan to attack the West. This was neither more nor less than a modern version of the 1914 invasion of France and consisted of destroying the allied army by entering through Belgium and advancing onto Paris (map 1.2). Basically, the strategy was to launch an offensive by turning around the northern flank, so that the Franco-German frontier could be avoided. In 1914 the Franco-German border was to be avoided because the bulk of the French army was concentrated there, and in 1940 because of the existence of the Maginot line, a costly and complex line of fortifications and defences which France had built along its borders with Germany and Italy after the First World War.

One innovator, Erich Von Manstein, had another plan (map 1.3). He knew that Germany ran the risk of a disaster similar to that of World War One, despite the fact that the army management was better prepared and had better tools available (tanks, aircraft, radio to coordinate attacks and keep the staff informed, etc.).

What did the experts think of innovator Von Manstein's suggestions? Something along the lines of what the experts said in 1975 when Bill Gates predicted the presence of "a computer in every office and every home, and Microsoft in every computer." In the words of Ken Olsen, the US engineer who founded DEC (Digital Equipment Corporation), at that time world leader in the IT world, "there is no reason for any individual to have a computer in his home."[4]

Map 1.2 The Schlieffen Plan 1914 / Yellow Plan 1940.

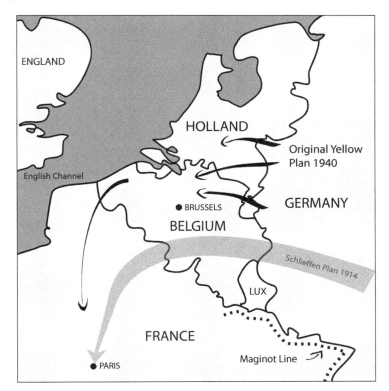

Fate played an important part in the events because, thanks to a series of coincidences, Hitler came to hear of Von Manstein's ideas, and in a move to confirm his authority over the High Command, he decided to adopt the business plan proposed by the innovator.

So what was his proposal? In contrast with the advice of the High Command experts (or Board of Directors, if you like), Von Manstein suggested that the centre of gravity should be located in the southern wing, opening a front where the enemy was weakest. The German army would advance towards the English Channel instead of Paris, thus capturing the French and British in a deadly trap by means of a pincer movement.

The plan had the added advantage that the French and British experts would think that the Germans were going to repeat the 1914 move and would place the entirety of their armies in Belgium, thus leaving themselves open to being surrounded, if Manstein's plan had worked.

Map 1.3 The Manstein Plan 1940.

The weak point of the Allies' layout was the Ardennes, a forested area with low mountains which both Allied and German experts considered unsuitable for armoured columns. If the Germans were fool enough to attempt an advance in that zone, the Allies felt that the artillery bombardment and other evidence of an offensive would give them sufficient time to react.

The Germans had one strong point in their favour. They were equipped with a very good product on which they could depend in their strategic development: the German Armed Forces.

As a general rule, a better product (a better Army in this case) does not automatically mean success (reach targeted market share, profitability or win a war) JVC was ahead of Sony when both companies came face to face in the analogue video format war. Sony had better technology and objectively the BETA system was superior to VHS, yet it was the latter system which triumphed and became universal. Something of this nature had occurred between 1914 and 1918 when the Germans, with a better product, were unable to win the war.

In 1940 the "classic" German army product (discipline, sense of duty, tenacity, initiative and competent officers) was reinforced by a new ingredient, a new method of fighting: The *Blitzkrieg* or the lightning war.

The *Blitzkrieg* strategy is based on three fundamentals:

1) Tanks, grouped in independent units, would advance *en masse* and become involved in their own battles without worrying about the infantry divisions which would be following at a distance, mopping up pockets left behind and consolidating the conquered territory. The armoured units were equipped with motor vehicles and supported by protected infantry (which was transported in armoured vehicles).

2) Once the tanks were deep in enemy territory they would no longer be supported in advance by the classical artillery bombardment, because this would slow down any advance. Artillery was now replaced by air support used on a huge scale to bomb enemy positions, interrupting communications and supply lines and preventing enemy reinforcements from being brought up.

3) Attacks were synchronised and coordinated by radio communications, since radios could be fitted in any vehicle or aircraft, and communications could be coded and decoded at high speed.

The result was a speed of advance never seen before, war at lightning speed, the *Blitzkrieg*!

The implementation of the Von Manstein business plan was placed in the hands of two officers. As Commander-in-Chief of the group of armies responsible for pressing home the main attack, an expert was chosen, Von Rundstedt, famous for his ability to see past the unnecessary, and the fact that he allowed his subordinate officers to act on their own initiative when required. In his memoirs, Von Manstein himself recalled that Von Rundstedt "a latent soldier who grasped the essentials of any problem in an instant. Indeed, he could concern himself with nothing else, being supremely indifferent to minor details."[5]

In the front line of the armoured troops was Heinz Guderian, a genuine innovator. He had been one of the inventors and main theoreticians of *Blitzkrieg*, and in Poland he had been given the job of putting it into practice for the first time. *Blitzkrieg* was still a modern version of war involving troop movements, but with aircraft and tanks based on a set of concepts as useful for war as for our day-to-day business situations: concentration, manouver, speed, mission command and vision.

2.1 Concentration

There can never be too much strength at the crucial point. When a strategy is established, it is appropriate to choose a point of maximum force, maximum gravity, a pivotal point at which we can launch our resources and from where we dismantle the defences of the enemy at our leisure.

In order to achieve this maximum concentration of resources, it is sometimes necessary to strip other fronts, leave other troops without supplies, to make room, because anyone who is not prepared to do this will never be able to make himself sufficiently strong at the crucial point.

When Procter&Gamble sold its less profitable brands (Sunny Delight or the deodorant Sure), what it was doing was freeing up resources, concentrating its troops on the most promising fronts (the major growth segments, those with greater profitability potential, with fewer competitors). The same applies to the situations when Duracell or Braun growth stagnated, with less investment devoted to them so that other businesses could be favoured.[6]

One fine day their great competitor Unilever realised that it owned 1,600 brands, but 63% of its income came from a mere 50. What was the High Command's decision? To concentrate resources on

40 brands, its so-called global brands (Dove, Knorr, Lipton, etc), which were supplied with huge amounts of resources to guarantee competitiveness at global level. The rest were classified into two groups: 360 were retained for the battle at the local level; while the remainder, 1,200 brands, were merged, sold off, removed from the catalogue, or simply allowed to die.[7]

Summing up, to achieve concentration you have to have a point of maximum force application: we need tree-trunks, not woodchips.

2.2 *Manouvre*

Break through the enemy's defences and advance. Attack where he least expects you, or, at least somewhere where he's not to be found. To achieve the desired breakthrough, both imagination and surprise are very desirable, but the essential condition is concentration.

In the case we're looking at, manoeuvring, the Germans found a breakthrough point, where the German forces were concentrated, where the enemy least expected them, and where they were likewise at their weakest: the Ardennes.

A German proverb says that a chain lasts as long as the weakest link. Strangely, when we intend to launch a product to drive a competitor out of the market, the natural tendency of the initial impulse is to face him where he's strongest. It's as if we've been dazzled by his success and that makes us want to fight on his ground. We feel a need to come to grips, failing to realise that maybe, with a little imagination, we can cut budgets, investments and waste, and guarantee ourselves at least the minimum conditions for success.

The Honda case is interesting. When it began to sell its products in the USA, it preferred to ignore the huge automobile market (a profitable, developed and still expanding market, and one in which there were huge competitors). It made its move in a small niche market, motorcycles (easy to produce, fewer parts, and of less interest to the automobile industry) and began to work via small scale sales initiatives. By 2006 Honda was selling more than one million four hundred thousand four-wheel vehicles in the US and Canada.[8]

2.3 Speed

As long as we're in motion, the enemy is paralysed, disorientated, finds it difficult to concentrate his resources in a definite location. As Guderian said in his memoirs, "The French found it difficult to direct their reserve corps as long as we were in motion".[9] Were the Germans headed for Paris or the English Channel? Constant motion is the key to preventing the opposition from knowing where we are, to avoid he can bring reinforcements from everywhere, for weakening and paralysing his defence system.

The fact is, that once the enemy knows where we're going, he can establish fortifications and protect himself. And then something which could have been taken swiftly in one fast action ends up costing rivers of blood, sweat and tears.

Beyond that front which is stiff with obstacles and fortifications, crowded with competitors armed to the teeth, dug into their trenches and protected by their big guns, there are open spaces, uncluttered green fields where our tanks can speed through at twice the normal speed and with half the casualty rate. Out there is what W. Chan Kim and Renée Mauborgne call the *Blue Ocean* (business ideas at this precise moment unknown), where there is no competition, where the water is not stained with the blood of struggling competitors, the blood which identifies the red oceans (high competition markets).

Of course, speed is risky – we have to leave our flanks unprotected, we may run out of fuel, we may be cut off from our bases, but these are calculated risks, risks we accept for the advantages we gain. Again, all too often taking no risks is the riskiest approach.

The history of business is littered with examples: any number of companies have started out to conquer markets at *Blitzkrieg* speed using unknown paths, occupying niche after niche, with negligible effort, driven only by the thought of how much they can press their sales forward each quarter.

The second you stop, your big competitors appear, with their well-trained teams of experts, their heavy financial artillery and their cash-flow weaponry. Who could have imagined in 1997 that it would be Google and not Microsoft who would lead internet development? Once we've broken through the front, run, baby, run!

2.4 Mission command (delegation/empowerment)

Leaders must trust their staff, as they have to depend on their initiative, experience and knowledge. The Germans referred to this as mission tactics, *Auftragstaktik*, and management gurus re-christened it delegation of powers, or empowerment. Every soldier in the German army was trained to take over the duties of his superior officer, in order to be ready to do so should it become necessary.

Originally developed by the Prussian army in the nineteenth century and now the official NATO doctrine, mission command basically means that headquarters only establish the objectives of a mission, while it is up to the officers in the field to decide the best way to achieve them.

This doctrine not only contributed to the first and spectacular victories won by the Germans, but it also caused the destruction of Germany to be long drawn-out and expensive. The Germans revealed a remarkable ability to give a good account of themselves, often when seriously short of material and human resources. As we shall see, however, there were many serious opponents of this doctrine among the High Command experts, as well as the armies in the field, including the *Führer* himself (this was the title adopted officially by Adolf Hitler, literally "the Chief").

Everybody who has ever held any position of responsibility in a company will have experienced interference from other members of the organisation, individuals who feel driven to give orders about the most petty of details, causing procedures to become inflexible, giving rise to misunderstandings, complicating operations and damaging results.

The duty of the best kind of manager is to ensure that his staff are suitably trained and adequately resourced, and to define strategic directions and objectives. But that kind of manager will also allow the troops in the field to take their own decisions. No general may allow himself to behave like a lieutenant, however much in the past he may have been the very best of lieutenants, the most prepared and the bravest. A general should allow his lieutenants to do their work while he concentrates on his – that is the guarantee of achieving the best results.

In 1974, Mohamed Yunus, a Bangladeshi businessman, felt moved to try to do something to lift his countrymen out of poverty, even though he might only be able to help a few of them. Flying in the face of the orthodox theories of experts, he decided to make personal unsecured loans of small sums of money to 43 women to give them an opportunity to undertake craftwork projects. His decision was to rely on these people to find the best way to pay the loan back, and assume that they would take responsibility for it.

The loans were paid off, and the interest generated now meant that further credit could be financed. By 1983 the project had grown to such a size that a bank had to be set up, what is now known as the Grameen Bank, the People's Bank. By 1996 the bank was operating in 36,000 villages with 12,000 on the payroll. In a country where the loan repayment rate is barely 30%, the Grameen Bank boasts a rate of 98%.

In 2006 the Grameen Foundation, founded by the bank, had a presence in 22 countries and it is assessed that credit has been extended to 11 million people.

What is the secret? Self-employment is the objective of microcredit and rests on a philosophy: "Every human being is capable of achieving more than he himself realises, if he can only manage to liberate the energy trapped within himself by resignation and habit."[10] Mission command pure and simple.

2.5 Vision

Perseverance means never losing sight of our objectives and keeping true to the origin of the action and its purpose. We must strive to keep a clear view of our plan from the outset, and stay faithful to it to the end, to avoid chasing after too many objectives at once, overrating the initial success and giving up original intentions.[11]

As we shall see throughout this book, many successes have come to grief because the will of whoever was called upon to lead has flagged at the last moment, or because at a particular time the leader has been dazzled by successes, and has abandoned the main goal in order to attempt to secure other secondary objectives which appear more within reach.

"History has proved that nothing is more difficult in war that to adhere to a single strategic plan. Unforeseen and glittering promise on the one hand and unexpected difficulty or risk upon the other, present constant temptation to desert the chosen line of action in favour of another."[12]

"In war, as in business, the true road to victory is not so much a matter of being successful; rather it is question of being unfazed by difficulties and setbacks."[13]

The Spanish multinational Freixenet bottled its first sparkling wines in 1914. But it was really only in 1965, with the arrival of Josep Lluís Bonet, that the company began to develop in a systematic way. One of the growth paths was international expansion. In this area, Bonet felt that success would arise from control of the British market: "Whoever wins the Battle of Britain, wins the battle of the world."[14]

He launched himself in this direction with a surge of activity and tenacity. For 20 years the company lost money through its British subsidiary until at last the market share was able to push the balance sheet into the black. By 2008, Freixenet was selling 200 million bottles in 150 countries, generating 70% of its income on international markets.[15]

But we must leave Freixenet's Battle of England for the moment and return to the Battle of France in May 1940. On the 10th the Germans invaded the Netherlands, Belgium and Luxembourg, thus launching the German offensive on the Western front.

With the agreement of all the experts, the Allied General Staff believed that this was a modern version of the 1914 plan. The Allied generals, World War One veterans all, believed that this time they would not be caught napping by the German advance.

"Frankly, we would be rather pleased if they launched an attack. We are ready for anything they can do"[16] the British Chief of General Staff had declared shortly before. "This time we shall not be fighting in France as we did in 1914. We shall establish a front in Belgium itself, hold the line there and France will not be invaded," the Franco-British General Staff experts reaffirmed.

The elite of the Allied army entered Belgium in search of the bulk of the German army. But they had plunged into the lion's mouth, because on the 12th, Guderian and his armour crossed the Ardennes. 72 hours later there was a 50 mile breach in the Allied line. The Germans advanced without pausing for breath and all attempts to concentrate troops to hold the Germans back were shattered by the German air force, the fearsome *Luftwaffe*. The Allies were taken aback. Where were they headed? Paris? The Channel?

They would be enlightened soon enough: on May 18th a Panzer division (Panzer is the name the Germans gave to their armoured vehicles) reached the English Channel. The elite of the Allied troops were trapped. By the 26th of May the French and British troops were close to disaster. They had failed to mount a counterattack. Facing them were the Germans advancing across Belgium; behind them the terrible Guderian who, once he had reached the Channel, swiftly wheeled right in search of the Allied rear.

The Allies were left with just one possibility – to try to evacuate their troops by sea in a bid to minimise damage. The units concentrated around the port and beaches of Dunkirk, and the question in everybody's mind was whether there would be time to escape before the Germans arrived. How many men could be saved? Maybe 50,000? If they couldn't manage that, the war would be over before the summer. Only a miracle could save them from catastrophe (map 1.4).

And miracles happen. You just have to believe in them. Nagged by insistence of the High Command, the *Führer* lost touch with his vision at the crucial moment, and ordered Guderian to hold his tanks back. Hundreds of miles from the front, the experts were deciding what was the best way to press home the battle in the field, and their decision was to rein in Guderian's war machine and let the troops who were advancing from Belgium finish the job.

Map 1.4 Allies defeated in Northern France (1940).

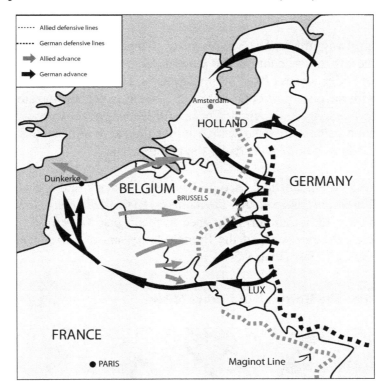

There is no shortage of reasons for such a decision (regrouping forces, resting the troops, preventing counterattacks, etc.). This kind of dynamic will never change: "intelligent people can always come up with intelligent reasons for doing nothing".[17] 48 hours later the order was countermanded, but it was too late, and it was all too obvious that ordering Guderian to rein in his advance had been a mistake.

During those two days the Allies had not wasted a moment and had managed to evacuate around 340,000 men, the bulk of the British Army, although they had been forced to abandon all their equipment (tanks, guns, vehicles, etc.) which would fall into the hands of the Germans.

Every day we have to take decisions, and it is not always easy to pick the right one. But once we have decided to follow a pathway, we must act with determination, regardless of the consequences. To hesitate is normal, but avoiding weakening and sticking to the strategy is usually the best way to ensure that victory does not slip away just when it is within our reach.

We can always think of a good reason to change our plans, always find an expert to advise caution, the kind of person who gets dizzy when they consider success. That's when we should assess the situation and stay with the plan, particularly if progress is as expected, and stop our ears to the song of the siren. Successful leaders never throw dice – they take calculated risks, which is not the same as foolhardiness, because taking no risks is really the greatest risk.

Once the trap had been closed in the north, France's fate was sealed: the *Wehrmacht* (theoretically the name given to all the German forces at the time, although normally used to mean just the Army) fell *en masse* on the remnants of the French Army, and it surrendered on June the 22nd 1940 (map 1.5).

Map 1.5 The Downfall of France (1940).

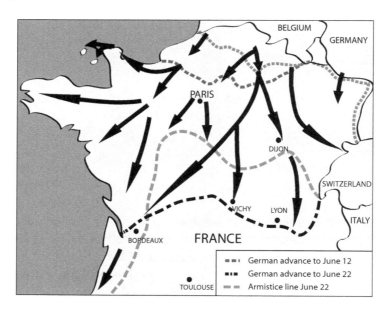

In just one month German soldiers had achieved what their fathers had fruitlessly attempted for four years two decades before. And the human cost had been infinitely smaller – the whole campaign cost the

Germans 45,000 dead and missing, while only the Battle of Verdun alone in 1916 had resulted in 100,000 dead.[18]

3 What to Do with a Sea Lion?

Once an armistice had been signed between France and Germany a very peculiar situation arose: neither Germany nor Great Britain knew what to do. France and Poland had fallen, Great Britain's army was in a state of collapse and totally lacked equipment (all its materiel was still in France), so if Germany could manage to land its troops on the island, the war was probably over.

But the Third Reich (the third German empire, following the Holy Roman Empire and Bismarck's empire), the name by which Hitler's Greater Germany was known, had no idea how to go about invading England. In the first place, its fleet was too small to face the British Navy, but worse than that was the fact that its leader was a morass of doubts and had no clear idea what he wanted to do.

On the one hand, it was obvious that occupation of the British Isles was crucial if any effort at reconquest by the Americans was to be avoided and victory was to be conclusive. But Hitler thought that there was a chance of reaching a rapprochement with the British, leaving him a free hand in Europe, saving him the work of an invasion. On the basis of this kind of thinking he put off making a decision until mid-July.

In actual fact, the most serious aspect of the German forces' situation was that their structure had no place for any high-level thinkers, apart from Hitler, focussing on defining clear strategic lines. And as far as Adolf Hitler himself was concerned, he had no technical background (his military experience consisted of courageous service as a corporal in World War one) and he lacked the time and training for the thinking that was required.

To make matters worse, it turned out that the plans of the German High Command's top experts were short term, with limited aims. Nobody had foreseen what to do, nor were there any proposals to be put to Hitler once Poland and France had fallen.

Once the war was over, both sides realised that Germany had no united and efficient control apart from Hitler. In his memoirs, Winston Churchill makes an eloquent summary: "The German High Command was very far from being a coordinated team working together with a common purpose and a proper understanding of each other's capabilities and limitations. Each wished to be the brightest start in the firmament."[19]

In order to maintain a vision, the only thing which is really essential is that you must have one. And to achieve that, the crucial issue is that there should be united command or one single head and one single direction. That head must have the ability to observe, analyse and finally to execute the plan in the face of unexpected difficulties and potential opportunities. This requires time and dedication.

As far as the British were concerned, the miracle of Dunkirk had not only rescued the majority of the British Army, but it meant that public opinion supporting the war had been reinforced. It would have been very difficult, even for someone with Winston Churchill's charisma, to justify a war with Germany if the whole British expeditionary force had been trapped in France.

Even so, the British were still forced to face the same problem as their enemy: "what should we do?" Great Britain and her colonies stood alone before the power of the Third Reich. Nevertheless, the will and inspired leadership capacity of their Prime Minister made the difference. What can we say about Churchill's management style?

In the first place, we should highlight his inspired optimism, creating unity from different intentions. In the wake of the terrorist bombing of the Twin Towers on September the 11th, 2001, Rudolph Giuliani, mayor of New York, quoted Churchill to remind everybody that "not even during the darkest days of the Battle of Britain did he emerge from Downing Street (the residence of the British Prime Minister) to say that he didn't know what to do, or that he was at a loss. He came out with a direction and a proposal, even if he had to make them up."[20]

The situation was very grave, and for one whole year (between the fall of France and the invasion of the Soviet Union) the British had to face the German war machine alone, taking heavy losses and gaining very little. Churchill offered "blood, sweat and tears", but above all he stood for a country united in the face of adversity, and he infused optimism into the hearts of those he was directing. As historian Andrew Roberts explains, Churchill was driven by the conviction that there is no doubt that those who feel part of a group face adversity better than those who feel isolated.

He also knew how to surround himself with constructive critics, accepted their counsel, centralised and organised the decision-making process. Tony Blair said that "the art of leadership means knowing how to say no, not yes". Nor did Churchill bear all the burden of command. Great Britain's Chief of Imperial Staff, Lord Alambroke, kept Churchill in check and complemented him. Hitler had nothing like this.

For Churchill, the best way to avoid strategic collapse in a war was to have a single controlling mind and a single decision-making power. This would cut down the number of committees, rationalising their decision-making powers, and keeping the number of solely consultative committees to a minimum: "What do you get when you put together the most valiant sailor, the most intrepid airman and the bravest soldier? The sum of their fears."[21]

He also liked to listen to other people's opinions. He was an exponent of what we call "management by walking about": he constantly visited factories, anti-aircraft batteries, anti-tank units and the like, often placing himself in difficult situation, as when he visited areas bombed by the German air force.

In his memoirs, when commenting on Churchill's management style, General Eisenhower said that to him, the Englishman was "an inspirational leader, he seemed to typify Britain's courage and perseverance in adversity and its conversatism in success… If he accepted a decision unwillingly he would return again and again to the attack in an effort to have his own way, up to the very moment of the execution. But once the action was started he had a faculty for forgetting everything in his desire to get ahead and invariably try to provide British support in a greater degree than promised."[22]

Finally we come to the third point, which is no less important: acting according to principles, moral values, with a desire to serve the ideas in which you believe. In his own words "a man's only guide is his conscience: the only shield his memory has is the rectitude and honesty of his actions. It is a great mistake to make your way through life unprotected by this shield, because on occasions the collapse of our hope and the inaccuracy of our calculations make fools of us; but with this shield, never mind how destiny plays out, we always march with the forces of honour."[23]

But let us return to the Battle of Britain. Faced with the British rejection of peace on German terms, the *Führer* had no other option than to order that a plan for an invasion of Great Britain be made. The German High Command experts swiftly got to work to frame the details of Operation Sea Lion *[Unternehmen Seelöwe]*.

The major obstacle was clearly the superiority of the British Navy on the seas, obviously much more powerful than any naval deployment the Germans could organise. Secondly, the British had preserved their Royal Air Force practically intact, and this was a fighting arm not to be dismissed lightly. And thirdly there were the survivors of the British Army, snatched from disaster in France in the nick of time, albeit very short of heavy weaponry and equipment.

Plans were made, and the conclusion was reached that an attempted invasion would only be possible if the Royal Air Force (RAF) could be neutralised, so that in the invasion the German Air Force *[Luftwaffe]* would be able to concentrate first on the Navy, and then on the Army, even though only temporarily. The most optimistic estimates were that they would need three days free of interference from the Royal Navy to successfully complete the first stage of the invasion. But the RAF had to be annihilated.

It was the Germans' bad luck that control of the *Luftwaffe* was in the hands of Hermann Goering. Goering had been a pilot and war hero during World War One, a loyal devotee of the Nazi cause from its tough beginnings, and he had been appointed a Marshal of the Reich. Such an impressive CV was not enough to conceal his obvious incompetence and the real reason for his promotion: his friendship with Hitler.

So along with the experts and innovators, we can now add a third type of manager – the incompetents, the specialists in doing things worse or more expensively, or doing them worse with the same resources. While a company may require experts and innovators in variable proportions, it is an undeniable fact that it really does not need the incompetents.

Everybody will at some time or another have met, and suffered, an incompetent manager. The worst thing about them is not that they have no idea how to do their jobs, nor that they are to be found in managerial positions. The real problem is that they will not give innovators any chance or let the experts do his work properly.

It is that not only do they allow no possibilities for innovators to operate, but they do not even permit the experts to do their work.

They undo the work of others and discredit it, bringing nothing but chaos. As Albert Speer, the German Minister for Armaments and War, put it: "the actions of Goering (in reality, of any incompetent) usually gave rise to total confusion, because he never bothered to thoroughly examine problems and his decisions were usually based on impulse assessments."[24] Incompetents lie frequently and knowingly, speaking with certainty on subjects they know nothing about, disqualifying and discrediting those who do know in front of the other members of the team.

For a variety of reasons, companies are obliged to have incompetents in their ranks, sometimes even in positions of great responsibility. What is the best way to neutralise them? You can even allow them to become Marshals of the Reich, but they must be prevented from accumulating any executive power, or at the very least, their power to stultify the dialectic struggle between experts and innovators must be reduced.

It is a fact that, on certain occasions, incompetents may be temporarily necessary (for example, political power can be granted to someone so that they will be neutralised in an interdepartmental battle). But anyone who knowingly awards a position to an incompetent must do everything they can to remove the content from this position so that real responsibility is limited.

With well-trained, battle-hardened pilots, good aircraft, modern tactics and commanded by generals who were aviation experts, the *Luftwaffe* put its shoulder to the wheel. The decision was to concentrate all efforts on attacking RAF airfields, to destroy the greatest number possible of aircraft on the ground, along with their facilities – radar stations, supply depots, etc.

The British were inferior in terms of aircraft numbers and pilot training, but on the plus side, they had an excellent fighter plane, the Spitfire, and radar, used for the first time in a war situation, which allowed them to concentrate resources where they were most needed, and on occasions, beat off the Germans' surprise attacks. They also had lookout stations all along the coast and they were playing at home, so that many pilots who were shot down could simply make a parachute landing and return to the battle once they had recovered from their injuries.

The battle began at the end of July 1940 and some kind of balance was maintained (both sides taking heavy losses) until mid-August when, thanks to attack operations by large formations of German aircraft on the British air force land installations, the *Luftwaffe* had the RAF on the ropes.

By the end of August, the British were on the brink of collapse. Lost aircraft greatly outnumbered new aircraft being produced and the commanders estimated that the supply of fighter planes would be exhausted within three weeks.[25] It looked as though, in spite of everything, German was going to get her own way.

And then the unexpected happened. On August 24 a few bombs fell on London by mistake. Churchill grabbed the opportunity, and, maybe just to boost British morale, decided to bomb Berlin on the same day that the Soviet Minister for Foreign Affairs, Molotov, had been invited to talk about the share-out of the world after the Britain's empire had been destroyed.

The air-raid sirens began to howl just at the moment when the Germans were trying to convince the Soviets to allow the Germans to place Europe in their sphere of influence in return for the increase in influence the Russians would gain in Asia at the cost of the British Empire. The Russian chancellor couldn't help making a comment, and as they hurried to the safety of the air-raid shelter, exclaimed, "if the British have been destroyed, then who is bombing us?"[26]

Damage was slight. But the German leaders lost their vision and set aside their strategic objective to concentrate on a secondary one; to avenge the bombing of the German capital with attacks on cities and civil objectives. Just when they were about to win the game, Germany tossed in its hand.

With the vision lost, the point of maximum effort was also abandoned, and the breakthrough point shifted to where the enemy had an advantage. Yet again, as we see in our daily work in the office, like a bull in the bullring, we throw ourselves at the cape, failing to work out how this works in favour of the bullfighter who awaits us, sword in hand.

The RAF won a desperate respite: airfields were repaired and the air squadrons were concentrated in an effective way against the German incursions. Soon the number of German losses (pilots and aircraft) began to show that the desired and essential air supremacy which had existed at first, had been transformed into nothing more than a dream.

The British began to swing the balance in their own favour, albeit at the cost of losses among the civilian population. The changing picture was not ignored in Germany, where voices began to be raised calling into question the opportunity of invading. The abandonment of daylight attacks because of their high cost flagged the High Command decision, formalised on October the 12th 1940, to cancel the invasion plan.

That summer, the RAF saved Great Britain. As Winston Churchill put it, "never was so much owed by so many to so few." If he had had all the data to hand, he probably would have included Hitler and Goering, since their tactical errors were so helpful in dragging the British out of the mire.

Like so many managers throughout our careers, the British Prime Minister, looking back over the period, arrived at this conclusion:

"When I look back on all these worries, I remember the story of the old man who said on his deathbed that he had had a lot of trouble in his life, most of which had never happened. Certainly this is true of my life in September 1940. The Germans were beaten in the Air Battle of Britain. The overseas invasion of Britain was not attempted. In fact, but this date Hitler had already turned his glare to the East. The Italians did not press their attack upon Egypt…we found means to reinforce Malta before any serious attack from the air was made upon it, and no one dared to try a landing upon the island fortress at any time."[27]

Stay true to the project and never be demoralised by troubles which may never really become problems, because maybe the Germans, despite what we think, are not going to invade us, and the fearsome Italian enemy may be no more than a paper tiger. The Italians? Yes… bear with me, and read on

2

Interval: the Balkans, Greece and the Mediterranean

1. A new Caesar is born: Benito Mussolini

We may be familiar with the example: a company is the absolute leader in its own country partly because of decades of clinging to a more-or-less captive market. Then one fine day, fired by some up-to-date news, the company decides to launch itself onto some fresh markets. The basic reasons are easy to understand: on the one hand we have the ambitions of the Chairman, and on the other the mistaken belief that the difficulties being experienced by others are the best guarantee of his success.

But reality is stubborn, and the weakness of your competitor is no automatic guarantee of your own strength. On more than one occasion the Chairman has ended up bankrupt, publicly shamed, and the company has lost its privileged position even in its captive market. This was what happened to Benito Mussolini and Italy during the Second World War. His mistake? Ignoring reality and allowing himself to be blinded by ambition. (Which was to result in his being murdered by partisans in 1945 along with his lover, their bodies being dangled from hooks on show in a public square). Before the invasion of Poland the Italians had hastily declared themselves non-belligerent, in other words, they did support the German side but without actually declaring war on Britain and France. They waited until June 10 to join in the conflict, when, just before the collapse of France, Mussolini decided to declare war on the Western Allies. The way he read the situation was that they were faced with an excellent business opportunity which would make it possible for them to make huge profits at very low cost.

After the fall of France, and expecting an invasion of England in the very near future, the Italians decided to conquer Egypt, a British protectorate, the key to the Middle East, and the doorway to Asia. The attack was to be launched from Libya, which at the time had been an Italian colony since 1912.

The Italian troops set out in September 1940. Italy, however, was no Germany and apart from being short of equipment and training, her troops had no stomach for the fight. Few officers were experts of any kind, innovators were scarce and incompetents were in charge on all sides.

The strength of the Army was, in any case, nothing more than a façade, a fact which the Italian bosses were well aware of, but dazzled by the glory which the conquest of Egypt would mean, they decided to turn a blind eye to realistic information and turn Mussolini into a new Julius Caesar.

Success would appear to have been a certainty, since facing the 250,000 men of the Tenth Italian Army were a mere 35,000 British troops. But in spite of numerical superiority, progress was modest, and once they had reached Sidi Barrani (some 65 miles inside the Egyptian border), the Italians halted to await "reinforcements" (at the time, the campaign was barely a month old). The British had merely withdrawn in good order on land. At sea, however, they inflicted serious losses on the Italian fleet and neutralised Italian maritime superiority, essential for getting supplies through to both sides. With September over, the British began to receive reinforcements, expecting a second Italian onslaught aimed at Cairo. The summer was melting away, and the Germans were making no efforts to invade Great Britain after all, which mean that Churchill had spare men he could use to consolidate his position in the Mediterranean. When *Il Duce*, name given to Mussolini (faced with a lack of progress in

Africa) decided to invade Greece in October, the British started to wonder what they could do, given the lack of military activity in Egypt. The High Command decided on a limited counter-attack to reinforce the British defensive positions and two divisions were thrown against a section of the Tenth Army's defensive system.

In barely two weeks the British advanced 560 miles and captured 130,000 prisoners, 380 tanks and 845 pieces of artillery. British losses were 500 killed, 1,400 wounded and 56 missing[1]. With noticeable sarcasm, the British Minister for Foreign Affairs paraphrased Churchill's famous sentence following the Battle of Britain to sum up the success of the campaign: "Never has so much been surrendered by so many, to so few."

With Egypt re-conquered and a large part of Libyan territory invaded, British advances in Italian colonial Africa were unstoppable, and were followed by Ethiopia and Somalia. On February 3 El Agheila was captured, a strategic position at the head of the Cyrenaic Peninsula on the north-east coast of Libya. At that early date in 1941 there was a real possibility that the whole of Libya might fall into the hands of the British, with the Italians driven from the African continent once and for all. What might be the consequences of this brilliant British success? Perhaps Italy would reconsider the situation in the light of such a humiliating collapse and decide to surrender, thus forcing the French colonies (at the time under the control of the collaborationist Vichy government)[2] in Morocco, Algeria and Tunisia to fall into the hands of the British.

But that hypothesis was not to come to pass. Now it was the British turn to make mistakes. They scattered their forces in search of simultaneous objectives, and this tactic meant that they were unable to achieve any of them. In February 1941 when they were on the point of giving the *coup de grace* to Italian control of Libya, Winston Churchill and his General Staff decided that the Cyrenaic region should be retained as a secure flank with the minimum force available, and the remaining available troops were to be sent to Greece. Greece? Yes – as we mentioned, Mussolini, committing a flagrant error of calculation, not content with his modest action in Egypt, decided in October 1940 to invade Greece. The conquest was yet another disaster, since not only had the Greeks repelled the invasion, but they had forced the Italians to withdraw, chasing them as far as Albania. As the Italians retreated, it became obvious that the Germans would have to intervene directly to save their unfortunate allies' bacon.

Map 2.1 North Africa in 1939.

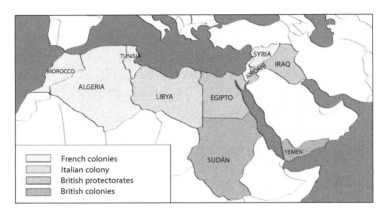

Great Britain was now faced with her own dilemma. Should she immediately hasten to the aid of the Greeks against the Germans, or was it preferable to finish the job in Libya first, and then go to the help the Greeks? The solution turned out to be mid-way between both. They would stop the Germans in Greece while still holding onto their positions in Libya. There would be time later to finish off the Italians.

It was the Prussian military theorist, Carl Von Clausewitz, held to be the father of modern military strategy, who said that "for in such dangerous thing as War, the errors which proceed from a spirit of benevolence are the worst."[3] Not only would the British be little help to the Greeks, but they were to be harassed by a fearsome enemy: the Afrika Korps.

2. Der Afrika Korp and its Managing Director

One of the great paradoxes of the Second World War in the case of Germany is her allies, who, instead of turning into a bastion of support ended up as a headache, weakening German positions. In other words, faced with the Allies determination to fight a coordinated war founded more or less on good faith, to be carried to its ultimate consequences, Hitler's main allies preferred the notion of "Parallel War" (in the words of Benito Mussolini himself). This meant that both Italy and Japan were prepared to wage war on the western powers, but would be doing so independently, without consulting Germany, pursuing their own interests and objectives, and with fatal results for all.

Every day we see similar cases in our businesses, where departments or general sections that know they are strong, with adequate resources and which open parallel fronts aiming to achieve their own objectives taking no account of the rest of the company. They forget the principle of unity of command (a single head and a single management) and think that a good product, huge resources and the best professionals are enough to win the war.

And this is all the more serious in the case of commercial partnerships. When two companies form an association, they must act in a coordinated way, with good faith, not seeking exclusively their own personal interests, respecting the letter and the spirit of the agreements. Parallel wars can work for a while, but they collapse in the face of an enemy equipped with a highly coordinated high-output system.

If you remember, we had left the British halted at El Agheila on February 9 1941, some 375 miles from the capital of Libya, Tripoli (the conquest of which would have meant the expulsion of the Italians from the African continent) with the cream of her troops on the way to Greece. In the meantime, Germany had been forced to intervene to help the Italians who, because of their own mistakes, were about to collapse on the fronts on which they were fighting. Hitler decided to send a small expeditionary force to Africa to back up the Italians. The German experts set to work and created the famous German Afrika Korps, placing at the head of the newly-formed force a certain Erwin Rommel, whom the British would later dub the *Desert Fox*.

Erwin Rommel was another of the great innovators of the German Army. He had already made his mark in the First World War, and in the new war he had been in command of the tanks which had conquered France. This is how Heinz Guderian praises him in his memoirs: "Rommel was not only a sincere, frank personality and a brave soldier, but he was also a very gifted leader. He possessed energy and tact, under the most difficult of circumstances he always found a way out, he had guts and he was devoted to his profession."[4]

There is not doubt that Rommel was a magnificent strategist, able to find new directions in each situation, his movements always revealing skill in manoeuvre and speed, and he was also capable of recovering from adversity and disaster. As a human being, he displayed nobility of character and the highest of ideals both for his men and for prisoners and civilians.

Another important quality of the German marshal was his ability to motivate his men by his own example. Mario Alonso Puig, in "Leadership Material", states that leaders "are leaders not because they strive to be first, but because they are the first to strive, and they do it in circumstances which are not easy."[5] The soldiers of the Afrika Korps put it another way: "nothing to the right; nothing to the left. Rommel straight ahead."[6]

On February 12th the Afrika Korps disembarked in Tripoli and in a month had built up its forces with the incorporation into its base of the Fifth Light Armoured Division. Rommel took stock of the situation and started to work without waiting for circumstances to become ideal given that they might never do so.[7]

Without his complete second division (the Fifteenth Panzer) and with the remains of the Tenth Italian Army he hurled himself against the British on April 1 with a violence and energy which astonished the German High Command as much as it did the enemy. In a fortnight the British had fallen back 220 miles and Rommel had reached the city of Tobruk, a strategic point for the development of the campaign. In this coastal city the Afrika Korps met fierce resistance and divided its forces to continue the siege while ploughing deeper into Egypt.

The *Luftwaffe* had made its appearance in the Mediterranean, cancelling out British superiority at sea and putting the Royal Navy on the defensive for the first time since Italy joined the war (map 2.2).

Map 2.2 Libya and Egypt (1940-1942).

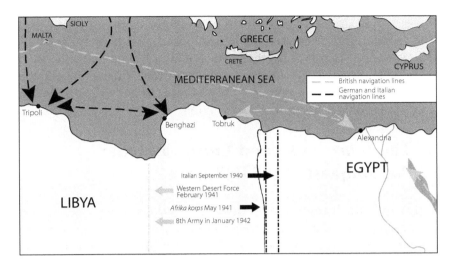

The war in the sands of North Africa presented two important peculiarities. The first was the importance of controlling the southern flank, the desert, which was essential to be able to outflank and surround the enemy. There were almost no natural obstacles to the movement of large mechanised formations, so that the side which managed to break through the southern flank held the winning hand.

The second feature was the ability to bring supplies up to the front, and in sufficient quantities, which was in itself a great competitive advantage. The best way to do this was to control the ports and the sea lanes. Because if provisioning by sea was impossible, and since there were also no railways, supplies had to be brought up by lorry. This gave rise to obvious risks since the need to cover large distances in extreme conditions was exacerbated by exposure to a situation of great vulnerability to attacks by enemy aircraft.

This situation meant that the port of Tobruk was the key to the possibility of advancing on Egypt. Without Tobruk, Rommel's supplies would have to arrive by road from Tripoli (a distance of some 1,100 miles) and to a lesser extent from Bengasi (600 miles). In addition to this the rear of the Afrika Korps was also in danger, threatened by the expected British counter-attack. Tobruk was too important a point to be left alone. He launched a number of assaults, but the fortress (well fortified and supplied by sea) resisted.

The German-Italians were unable to proceed, and their fruitless attempts to take Tobruk, plus their time spent in Egypt, had exhausted them. They stopped. The moment arrived for the British to launch the counter-blow they had prepared. It was now June 1941 and Operation Battleaxe was about to go into action.

3. The *Führer*'s second European tour: the conquest of the Balkans (1941)

Just as in Hitler's case, Benito Mussolini's virtues as a politician and his populist allure and charisma had no equal in the world of the military genius. And as also with the *Führer*, the Italian leader was not prepared to yawn his way through the advice of experts or innovators. On October 28th 1940, with his African adventure hanging in mid-air, *Il Duce* decided to invade Greece from Albania (which the Italians had occupied in 1939).

The Italians were expecting a military picnic by way of the conquest of the Hellenic peninsula, but the Greeks, as we have already seen, far from being daunted (one anecdote recounts that, in the initial skirmishes, an Italian soldier turned to his superior officer and stammered: "Excuse me sir, but the Greeks are shooting at us!"), first resisted and then counter-attacked, forcing the Italian army to retire. By mid-December the Greeks were in possession of a quarter of Albania.

In March 1941 the Italians launched a counter-offensive which was a stupendous failure. This was what brought the Germans onstage. It was one thing for the Transalpine troops to fail in Africa, but it was quite another for the Germans to put up with an Axis collapse on European soil. The German army prepared for action.

On April 6th the German army burst into Greece and Yugoslavia. 20 days later Athens was in German hands. The British troops, so needed in Africa where they could have completely tipped the balance, were barely able to offer any resistance to the Germans and withdrew from the European continent for the second time in one year.

Hitler decided to invade Crete to prevent it being used as a base to bomb the continent, particularly the Romanian oil wells. To occupy the Mediterranean island he used his paratroopers, and although the suffered more casualties in ten days than in the entire conquest of the Balkans, the south flank was secured just in time for the next great challenge of the German Armed Forces, the *Werhmacht*.

3

Barbarossa: the World Will Hold its Breath

At 4.00 am on June 22th (by a strange coincidence almost the same day on which the Napoleonic armies invaded Russia), 1941, the Germans unleashed what was known as Operation Barbarossa: the invasion of the USSR (the Union of Soviet Socialist Republics), the old Russian empire now under new management, the Communists.

Only hours before, Hitler had remarked that with the launch of Barbarossa "the world will hold its breath and make no comment."[1] Indeed, in terms of troop numbers, resources and the size of the combatants, this was the greatest military confrontation ever. The struggle was to be violent and brutal, almost unparalleled on other fronts.

Naturally, the invasion plan had been Adolf Hitler's own idea. At the zenith of his triumph, in the summer of 1940, aware that he was unable to invade England, he decided to deal with another player still at the table, the Soviet Union. He may well have thought that this was the best moment to unleash this storm. He believed that at that time the USSR was very weak, so that with Great Britain out of action and the United States far from being able to become involved in the war, Germany would arise as the major world superpower.

It was a risky decision because it meant a war on two fronts, anathema to military theorists and the main reason for the failure of Germany during the First World War. The invasion of Russia had also been the cause of Napoleon's downfall in 1812.

Rather than a calculated risk, it looked more like a throw of the dice in the hope that luck would be on his side yet again.

1. Barbarossa: the Business Plan

In the words of Peter Drucker, "a plan is not something to be achieved, but something to be activated when it is not achieved."[2] Helmuth von Moltke *the Elder*, Prussian army general who destroyed the French in 1870 put it more succinctly – "no plan survives the first encounter with the enemy."

With Hitler's requirements in mind, the experts set to work. Overall, their plan was in the end too ambitious, imprecise and vague, its aim being to destroy the Red Army before the winter. The reality Von Manstein acknowledged in his memoirs was that it lacked "homogeneity as regards military and strategic objectives, both in the drafting and then in the execution."[3]

But the experts' studies, far from discarding it as illusory, vain or risky, supported Barbarossa to the extent of courting direct disaster.[4] The foundations it was based on were unrealistic, but they provided the plan that *the Führer* wanted to hear, based on excessively optimistic criteria which underestimated an enemy who had to be defeated in a very short space of time in a huge theatre of operations.

Does it ring any bells? More than likely. You must at some time have been presented with a detailed and extremely ambitious plan for the upcoming financial year, with all the objectives carefully explained. It seems that nobody was about to openly express doubts or hesitations regarding any of the aspects. And yet the very first time the team met informally, everybody said that it would be impossible to achieve all the objectives. When people ask us about the weak points, we normally prefer to reserve our criticisms, keeping our comments to doubts of a purely technical nature, and avoiding going to the heart of the matter. As a general rule nobody quits or hands their work back to the management. And that means there's always someone cheeky enough to wonder "Why not?".[5]

When Hitler presented the Barbarossa plan to his generals, the reaction was similar. Faced with the operation, with all the doubts that his generals must have felt, all he heard was an approving silence. Nobody resigned, nobody pulled out, nobody was willing to tackle the wishes of Germany's leader. Guderian's memoirs put it as follows: "The meeting accepted Hitler's speech without protest, since there was no debate; the meeting broke up in silence, wrapped in the most serious of concerns."[6]

Optimism, ambition, the hope to be able to do things better than circumstances suggest – these are all qualities which will be required of a good manager. Being demanding of oneself is what leads to the achievement of great things, goals seen as perhaps unattainable are attained.

But the problem here is that the plan suffered from significant inconsistencies and calculation errors from the very outset, with the participants entrusting their success to a kind of cosmic fate which would make problems to solve themselves before they actually revealed themselves in all their glory. It can certainly happen, but we must be aware that it extremely unlikely.

There is a problem when no clear objectives which can be achieved with the available resources are defined. But that problem becomes serious when, once a given plan has been initiated, the strategic view is lost and opinion changes continually, regarding both apparent successes or possible failures.

Initially, the business plan consisted of meeting and destroying the Russian army via pincer movements, capturing the three major cities of the Soviet Union, Leningrad, Kiev and Moscow (in that order), and establishing a solid line of defence in the east while waiting for the soviet republics to collapse. Because of the vast extent of the country, a complete invasion was set aside as technically impossible (see map 3.1).

Map 3.1 Barbarossa: planned phases of invasion.

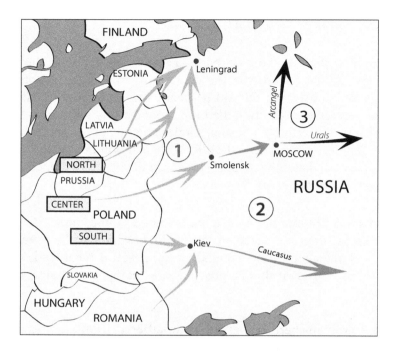

The Soviet Union was seen as a giant with feet of clay, a mish-mash of peoples and races crushed under the cruel jackboot of communism which would collapse when the main capital cities fell. But not only did the Germans take no advantage of this, despite their hopes being based on it, but the Nazi managers soon treated the Russian people so poorly that the hated communist authorities seemed, in comparison, jolly schoolboys.

And if that were not enough, the Germans now discovered that the military resources of the Soviets were much better than they had thought, both as regards men and the quality of their equipment.

Barbarossa is a paradigm of a painstakingly studied business plan with aggressive objectives. So far, so good, a foundation which would be accepted by any business school. However, even the most basic management textbook states that objectives must be ambitious, but achievable with the resources available.

The books will also say that goals must be simple and clear; and above all, that the main strategic actions must not change in the face of a combination of adverse events or brilliant successes.

I must insist on this: simplicity and clarity. Things will get complicated enough by themselves on the battlefield. Once again Von Clausewitz deserves quoting: "Everything is simple in War, but the simplest thing is difficult. These difficulties accumulate and produce a friction which no man can imagine exactly who has not seen War."[7]

2. Stalin and Hitler: two styles of management

Some people are incapable of delegating because they cannot bear things to be done in a way other than theirs.[8] The conflict between Germany and the Soviet Union was a battle to the death between two ideologies (national-socialism and communism), but also between two men (Adolf Hitler and Josef Stalin), and between two management styles.

In the first weeks of the invasion Soviet losses were immense – and avoidable. When Stalin saw the German tanks advancing at top speed towards the border, he thought it was a bluff. On May 15th, when he already had conclusive proof that the Germans were planning to invade the USSR, including intelligence about the date and time of the invasion, he rejected the idea suggested by some of his General Staff members who advised a preventive attack. With the German incursion under way, Stalin was overwhelmed for several days by a state of mental paralysis and deep depression. Racked by violent mood swings, he sacked some of his top military advisors.

Stalin's sluggish reaction and military incompetence, aggravated by his generals' fear and subservience and the limitations of the inflexibility of the Soviet strategic concept resulted in entire armies being found in exposed positions, easily trapped by the Panzer formations which were racing across Soviet territory.[9]

Even though the Russians possessed numerical superiority in terms of men, tanks and aircraft, German tactics and preparation meant that by autumn the Soviets had lost between three and six million men if you counted dead, wounded and captured. Because you do not have to be stronger to win, merely stronger at the decisive point (do you remember what we saw on the matter of the point of maximum effort?).

Even so, Stalin was a better organiser. On June 30th he set up a small war committee, the State Defense Committee. Initially with four members plus himself, the committee was set up with plenipotentiary powers and the right to override any procedures and bureaucracy. The members enjoyed Stalin's complete confidence, and they would have no hesitation in explaining a situation to him exactly as they perceived it; and they were undoubtedly endowed with great intellectual capabilities and the capacity for hard work. He was now provided with a very flexible organisation, one which could provide a more realistic picture, which was less bureaucratic and more able to react to changes.

At the military level, he took the position of supreme commander of the Soviet General Staff *[Stavka]*, so that he had a complete view of the realities on the home and external fronts.

As the war progressed, Stalin came to recognise his limitations as a military strategist and increasingly accepted the advice of his trusted advisors he learned to delegate to the military professionals. In spite of his huge ego, he was intelligent enough to know how to listen to and accept advice.[10] A word to members of steering committees: Zhukov, one of his main military advisors learned how to "convince" Stalin on a basis of firmness, clear arguments and a very firm grasp of details... remember that, the next time you have a meeting with your boss.

Stalin also understood that "regardless of preoccupation with multitudinous problems of great import, he must never lose touch with *the feel* of his troops."[11]

For this purpose, he would send direct representatives to various locations on the front so that they could describe what they saw and what they felt. He also had no hesitation in speaking directly to a general to encourage him, to emphasise the importance of the work he was doing, or stress what was expected of him.

And, finally he trusted his General Staff, delegating the planning and execution of military operations to them. In this climate of collaboration, where realities could be expressed simply and honestly, unadorned, the Soviet generals gained in confidence and resolution.

This system of organisation meant that he could concentrate on the home front where he had much more experience and knowledge about mobilising the Soviet Union's human and material resources, which in the end would be the key to victory over the Germans.

He applied his powerful will to motivating those around him and to directing their energies to the management of the war. He expected huge sacrifices from his suffering people, and he got them. The cult of the personality forged round the figure of Stalin in the nineteen-thirties meant that this became possible during the conflict. The Soviets were devoted to their leader and were prepared to make the sacrifices for him which he asked of them. To a certain extent, the Stalin cult was necessary to wage the war. He provided a focus where everybody could concentrate their loyalty and he stimulated an ever-increasing belief in the final victory.[12] It is impossible to ignore the brutality of the Soviet regime, but it is obvious that Stalin succeeded in motivating the peoples of the Soviet Union, body and soul, to the point of exhaustion.

The power structure in Germany was also very centralised and Adolf Hitler personified the highest military and civil authority, but this was not controlled in a coordinated manner. His work methods were chaotic, he encouraged rivalries between his subordinates and he changed his mind often.

As the war progressed, unlike Stalin and Churchill, Hitler's faith in his military abilities and his non-existent strategic genius grew continually. He imagined that his experience in the First World War as a corporal and his unbreakable will meant that he understood the dynamics of the war better than all the experts in the General Staff. He felt that his generals were too careful and conservative if not actually cowardly and untrustworthy.

When the first reverses and failures made their appearance, he heaped the blame on his subordinates and chose to take even less notice of them, to delegate less and to take on ever increasing responsibilities, rather than trusting in his generals. He became overwhelmed with work, insisting on personally taking all decisions at a certain level of importance. Doing this, he lost perspective on matters, but also he imbued the command structure with unnecessary rigidity, which was fatal in terms of strategy and tactics.

The *Führer* wasted energy on work for which he had no training, beyond his abilities, causing him to abandon the home front (see Chapter 6, "Other Fronts, Other Problems").

How often have we seen this in the business world? Good financial directors who, when they become managing directors, try to operate as sales managers, too, in the belief that their new position gives them experience and knowledge they do not possess. We should bear in mind that you can be an innovator and even a genius, but that doesn't automatically convert you into an expert, nor does it mean you can do without them.

Often in our professional lives we find ourselves being carried away by the allure of certain positions and responsibilities, because of the personal or professional prestige they imply. But a job or a position is just that, a name, and it does not enable us to do that job. It does not make us experts in everything, just as the fact of having been successful in the past does not make us infallible in the future.

3. It's Summertime and the Livin' is Easy

We had left some three million German soldiers on the morning of June 22th 1941. The attack was developed in three columns.

Army Group North, under the command of Field Marshall Ritter Von Leeb was essentially responsible for the advance from eastern Prussia onto the Baltic States. Their mission was to secure the ports and then fall on Leningrad (now Saint Petersburg) to join up with the Finns. Finland had been invaded by the Soviets in 1939 and after putting up stiff resistance had surrendered in 1940, yielding 10% of its territory to the USSR. In 1941 the Finns opted to win it back with German support. But throughout the entire length of the war Finland was very unwilling to fight outside of its 1939 borders, and ended up in a state of a sort of armed neutrality as far as the USSR was concerned.

The Central Army Group, under Fedor Von Bock, was to follow Napoleon's route to Moscow once it had defeather all the main concentrations of the Red Army in its path.

And finally, a third group, called South Army Group, commanded by Gerd Von Rundstedt, was to attack from the south with the support of the Romanians, aiming for Kiev. The goal was to secure the agricultural wealth of Ukraine and as far as possible the oilfields of the Caucasus.

The military plan was to repeat the *Blitzkrieg* – lightning war – which had been so successful for the German army in the past. In other words, with air superiority guaranteed, the armoured divisions would open the initial breaches with the aid of the infantry to then penetrate and surround the bulk of the enemy army, which, once trapped, would be annihilated by the infantry. Since the artillery would be following the infantry, the *Luftwaffe* would be acting as flying artillery for the benefit of the tanks.

At first, things went quite well. Spectacular advances were made and Soviet losses were huge. On June 26th, Minsk (the capital of Belarus) fell, and by July 16 they reached Smolensk (the first city inside the Russian republic, some 155 miles from Moscow) where the battle dragged on until August 8. The Central Army Group alone had managed to capture around a million prisoners, five thousand pieces of artillery and some nine thousand tanks.

In the north, progress was even faster. Von Manstein was advancing up to 50 miles a day, placing him halfway to Leningrad and allowing him to capture important bridgeheads on the river Dvina. 1,600 aircraft, 1,400 vehicles, and 4,000 pieces of artillery were destroyed, 35,000 prisoners were taken, and 90,000 Russians died. At the beginning of July, Saint Petersburg also seemed within reach.[13]

In the south, the German army met stiffer resistance and progress was less remarkable. On the one hand, they were faced by the toughest Russian forces, dug into good, indepth defense positions (instead of establishing one, very strong line, they set up a number of weaker ones, which make the enemy lose momentum, scatter their forces and slow the advance). And on the other, the advance had to bypass the Pripet marshes (an area of swamp and dense forest, with a low population and poor communications). But even so, by the beginning of July they had also achieved their objective and were at the gates of Kiev (map 3.2).

Map 3.2 Eastern Front (September 1941).

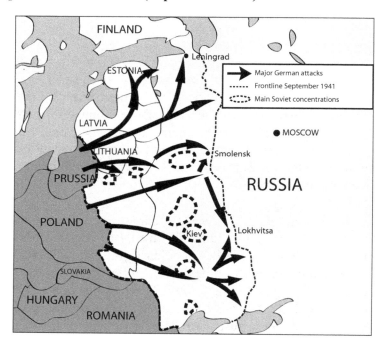

At this point the first tensions appeared. In the field it was now obvious that their objectives suffered from being enormously ambitious and that Nazi intelligence about the Soviet capacities were over-optimistic. It looked as though the Germans were not strong enough to move all three Army Groups forward at the same time.

Once again disagreement broke out between innovators and experts. The latter, almost always of superior rank, were uneasy about the security of their flanks which were too exposed, and the fact that the armour

60

was too separated from the infantry. It was not unusual for the Panzers to find themselves as much as sixty miles ahead of the infantry, which made it difficult for the infantry soldiers to seal off the pockets which were being produced. But the innovators knew that while the troops maintained the equation of *manouvre plus speed*, always concentrating on the point of greatest effort, it didn't matter that empty spaces were left behind them, as the enemy had everything to lose. The foe would be like a dismasted ship, unsteerable, uncertain what to do.

As we have seen, the worst thing which can happen is for the advance to grind to a halt, the front line is full of fortifications, sweat, mud and blood. We must look ahead, towards the green, open fields, the blue seas, because "Once it comes to a halt it will immediately be assailed from all sides by the enemy's reserves."[14] This dialectic between innovators and experts, egged on by a Hitler who was determined to control everything, with his General Staff also holding varying points of view, was an endless source of delays and lost opportunities.

Curiously, the marketing world experiences a similar debate, that which is generated by the launch (or non-launch) of products or services intended to protect the flanks of a brand from the attacks of the competition. The weakest flank of the mass consumer market products (Danone, Procter&Gamble, Apple, etc.) is usually the price, although others exist (a very fixed feature of the product, its positioning, distribution, etc.).

In situations like this, the experts advocate a defence of the flanks, by holding back in the innovation approach, and bringing out second quality products which might make up for some of the weaknesses of the more successful products. The innovators respond that what is required is an improvement in the current product, instead of wasting time by copying the competitors. We are leaders and it should be we who decide where the market is going.

Leaving flanks unprotected has its risks, but protecting them with specific products implies that the leader companies are sacrificing their vision, their *manouvre* and their resources to launching fighter brands and thus slowing down their advance by protecting their flanks, losing the competitive advantage which they had at the outset. In actual fact, most "fighter brands" or flankers usually end up as dismal failures.[15]

Apart from the above matters, the Germans had another problem of greater significance. Once the first stage had been completed with some degree of success, what was the next step?

Yet again there was no vision, no unity of command. The various heads of the Army and the General Staff disagreed among themselves, each conspiring against the others to impose his will. The supreme commanders pushed and pulled each other this way and that, and in turn tried to convince Hitler. The month they lost in these discussions gave the Soviets a respite which would ultimately prove decisive.

With Smolensk captured, the choices were to dash for Moscow or keep to the original plan (the Centre Army Group would divide into two parts: one would turn north to help with the conquest of Leningrad while the other would join the group laying siege to Kiev).

The discussion was long and confused. The conquest of Moscow, merely 150 miles from Smolensk, meant capturing the nerve centre of Soviet communications (which, in fact, would split the Soviet Union in two), and occupying the spiritual capital of communist Russia, as well as a first rank industrial centre. It was also, of course, the quickest way to destroy the Soviets, since it was obvious that the Red Army would sacrifice all available troops to its defence.

The capture of Kiev meant the conquest of Ukraine and also tied up significant Soviet troops, while it also avoided leaving a vast flank between the Central and Southern Army Groups groups open to the Soviets.

Ukraine was important because of its raw materials. In addition to this, overcoming the Crimea would prevent the Russians from bombing the Romanian oil wells on which Germany was largely dependent.

In the north, the occupation of Leningrad was the gateway to the domination of the Baltic by joining forces with the Finns (who were unwillingly fighting against the Soviets outside their own borders).

The Finns might then be persuaded to help Germany to attack the port of Murmansk, in the Arctic Ocean, some 100 miles from the Finnish border. The strategic importance of Russia's most northerly port in Europe was that a railway line went directly from there to Moscow along which travelled the supplies which the Russians were receiving from the Allies.

Although the majority of the generals were in favour of continuing to advance towards the capital, the *Führer* made it clear who was in charge in Germany, and personally ordered a section of the armoured divisions of Army Group Center to move south to capture Kiev, while another section would swing north to take Saint Petersburg.

The forces of Army Group Center headed south, under command of Guderian, joined up with South Army Group and in barely a month (between August 25th and September 26th of 1941), the Germans smashed the Soviet forces. The figures were devastating for the Russians: 665,000 prisoners, 880 tanks, 3,700 pieces of artillery and 3,500 motor vehicles destroyed.

But in the north, things were not going so well. Indecision and lack of vision were a serious drag on the German advance. In the first place, the July halt, 100 miles from Leningrad, had given the Russians time to build fortifications. In the second place, the troops of the Centre Group who were swinging towards the north were moving too slowly and in small groups. To cap these misfortunes, on September 4th the General Staff had changed its mind and had decided not to take Leningrad but to besiege it.[16] Even when they hastened to correct this decision it would already be too late.

Hitler believed that he was a great military leader, but really he was no more than a talented amateur who had been lucky. Guderian defined him as "daring, even reckless when it came to making plans, but timid when it came to executing them."[17] He was to make up for his lack of military genius with other qualities, such as his enormous willpower and an unusual memory for figures and statistics. In addition, his grasp of presentations and reports was extraordinary.

He was also clearly a first-rate master of oratory (the same quality which had helped him win the elections in 1933 and get into power), a gift which he knew how to adapt to suit his audience. He could recast his thoughts as clear formulae, and drive them home with his endless repetitions ("I shall never give up my Right", or "I shall never surrender!"). Generals of great experience, aware of their boldness and brave in the face of the enemy, crumbled under the effect of his speeches and fell silent before his arguments.[18]

Those constructive critics who were unswayed by his dialectics were speedily replaced by more easily-led individuals whom he handled with ease, paying little attention to their professional worth.

What is certain is that Hitler was neither an expert nor an innovator, no matter how hard he tried, but neither was he incompetent. He was more of a dreamer, like so many self-made businessmen are. The world of business has produced thousands of examples of people who start their businesses with nothing, and who without training or education build huge industrial empires.

Dream-weavers are able to see, to intuit, what lies beyond, but they often lack the skills or know-how to attain that vision. While an expert might try to do the same better, or an innovator to do so differently, a dreamer has no clear idea how to go about it, but he will allow himself to be led by his intuition, and a combination of work, luck, some social skills or actual technique, is often enough to achieve his first success.

But nobody should be deceived. In those successful cases we can all bring to mind, all the dream-weavers were capable, at some point, of stepping to one side and delegating the work to the experts and innovators, accepting their advice. Stalin realised in time; Hitler did not.

Hitler, like many other self-made businessmen, continued to trust his intuition, his luck, his feelings, whatever had always worked before. Faced with ever-increasing complexity, this was not enough, and disaster was inevitable when he refused to seek the support of good command structures.

The *Führer* had taken no professional military courses, nor was he skilled in the operations of the General Staff, his understanding of military technology was that of an amateur, and his military experience was very limited. He brought to High Command two concepts more appropriate to General Custer (one of the few US generals to be defeated by the Indians because of his irrational foolhardiness and his scorn for the enemy) than Clausewitz. The first was that the Army must continue on the offensive regardless of the circumstances. The second was no less suicidal – fighting till death rather than abandon ground.

Overwhelmed by the difficulties caused by their own actions, leaders such as these tend to turn in on themselves, hoarding increasing levels of power to themselves, aggravating the situation still further.

In the words of Albert Speer, Germany's minister of armaments and war production, "dilettantism was one of Hitler's peculiar characteristics. He had no actual occupation, and was basically a freelancer. Like many autodidacts, he was incapable of being an expert at anything, which meant that he was unable to appreciate the difficulties involved in any undertaking of importance, and he was constantly assuming new tasks. But again, as happens with many amateurs, he began to collapse when the first setbacks occurred. Then his ignorance of the rules of the game became a weakness and his tendency to improvise ceased to be an advantage.[19]"

When Bill Gates and Paul Allen created Microsoft in 1975, an unwritten rule stated that no employees should work for a boss who wrote worse computer code than they did. Just five years later, they hired Steve Ballmer as Chief Operating Officer. Steve had cut his teeth at Procter & Gamble selling soap, and obviously was no computer programmer.[20] In this case the dreamer Gates had no hesitation in delegating in an expert.

Bill Gates's success was rooted in his having dreamed that the computer business would live on high-volume, low margin business, realising that making hardware and writing software could be stronger as separate businesses. However, he figured out that his ability to see ahead did not automatically make him an expert or innovator when it came to doing business.

So he took on an expert, but not only in fields he could not master, but also in areas related to programming itself. He has never hesitated to imitate, buy or incorporate competitors, to surround himself, even in his own field, with capable people who could put him in the shade.

Saying this, if you happen to be a dream-weaver, why don't study an MBA? Even though it might be expensive and highly theoretical. Perhaps what the dream-weavers need is a touch of academic excellence to keep on moving forward. At college they might meet the experts who need their ability to dream. But, as a dream-weaver if you do not want to expand your education, just hire the talent! If you do so, remember, listen to them, at least once in a while, after all, you will be paying them.

4. Moscow: So Near, Yet So Far

The Battle of Kiev had hardly been opened when Hitler again changed his strategy and decided to take Moscow and merely to surround Leningrad. Once more, priorities were re-assigned and the point of maximum force shifted, troops had to be moved from one front to another, and the vision faded yet again.

So the original plan was transformed, driven by the fears of the General Staff, from Leningrad-Kiev-Moscow to Kiev-Leningrad-Moscow to finally settle on Kiev-Moscow-Leningrad (in the end it was only Kiev which was taken). Changing criteria and taking decisions based on apparent economic and political considerations confounded the military objectives of the operation, causing great losses of time and men and weakening Germany's position. But events continued to reward the *Führer* and his military genius. After the crushing defeat of Kiev, the troops of the Centre Group Army enjoyed a short rest, backtracked along the road they had followed towards the flanks and started on an anti-clockwise trajectory to make a grab at the jackpot, Moscow. This was Operation Typhoon.

October 12 witnessed the Battle of Briansk (250 miles south-west of Moscow) and Viazma (some 75 miles west of Moscow, a city which had been the shield of the capital on the occasion of previous attempts at conquest, where once again a huge quantity of materiel and prisoners were taken (over 600,000). Could Hitler be infallible? But what happened next was what everybody had thought might follow:

after the autumn came the winter. First the rain left the roads impassable because of the mud, then there was the ice and finally the snow. *General Winter* had made his terrible and inevitable appearance.

The lack of preparation on the part of the German Armed Forces for a phenomenon which was as expected and easily foreseeable as winter seems very surprising if not astonishing. For example, when the temperature dropped for the first time the troops were still in their summer uniforms, now threadbare after four months of marching and fighting.

Even more surprising was the inability of the General Staff to concentrate all its forces on a point of maximum effort; this was the decisive moment of the campaign, and doomed all the rest of the conflict for Germany. Instead of sending reinforcements to Russia, the Germans kept 34 divisions with nearly 900,000 men in Western Europe in readiness for a non-existent British threat, and scattered their forces over secondary theatres like the Mediterranean, where they sent a large *Luftwaffe* support contingent.

The Soviets did not waste a moment and between October and November 1941 they amassed 62 divisions in the Moscow front. At the same time and in the same front, all the reinforcements the Germans were able to send was a legion of French volunteers and a few paratroops. In an exercise of incomprehensible incompetence, they kept five divisions with nothing to do in Norway and Finland, soldiers properly equipped and trained to operate under winter conditions.[21]

The German armies were on the brink of exhaustion, the units decimated after months of hard fighting, and the human and materiel losses could not be replaced. The *Werhmacht* made one final lunge at Moscow lacking in any kind of mass manoeuvre or strategic reserve (a mass manoeuvre is a significant force kept protected to be used in the case of strategic necessity. For Clausewitz the purpose of the strategic reserve is the "prolongation and renewal of the combat and for use in case of unforeseen events. The strategic reserve is only to be used in the final stage of the battle.") Every unit was involved in the battle.

By way of a vicious circle that was difficult to stop, incomplete units meant more casualties than necessary, and more casualties than necessary meant more incomplete units, which in their turn generated more and more unnecessary casualties.

This hardly seemed to disturb the General Staff which, from its distance, was giving orders to move divisions over impracticable terrain to units which existed only on paper. Few people at the *Wolfsschanze* seemed to have any idea of the circumstances facing their troops. [Literally, Wolf's Lair – Hitler's headquarters during the greater part of the war, and located in what is now Poland. It was known as such because for a while the *Führer* was nicknamed Mr. Wolf by his close friends.] I must confess that I have experienced situations in the business world like this. Management is normally in favour of stretching resources to the limit, and placing little or no value on the foot soldier, assuming him to be replaceable or, even worse, dispensable.

It frequently happens that departments are called upon to operate with minimum resources, with staff workloads at breaking point and staff burnout on all sides. Not only does this mean that the work environment deteriorates, but it also leads to the first casualties (absenteeism, sickness, staff going over to the competition, and the like). The more the casualties, the lower the morale of those who remain, who are themselves likely to go down in the struggle.

We lose specialists hard to replace, staff we have trained, who know the organisation and the company, even though they are young; we lose petty officers, technical managers, etc. What is sad about this is that it is possible to avoid it relatively easily – all that is required is a little more attention to detail, some assurance that resources can be shipped in from other areas less overwhelmed by work, the issue of a few medals or rewards, and care that salary levels and worker wellbeing are appropriate.

It may be that while times are good and the markets kind, this kind of thing is relatively unimportant, as indeed, it was in Poland or France. But as soon as difficulties arise, the whole company will regret casualties which need not have occurred.

This is not just a theoretical exercise; treating employees well really impacts bottom line results for the company. As an example, it is calculated that the US software company SAS saves 85 million dollars per year on training and recruitment costs (as well as savings from absenteeism and sickness) thanks to this type of policy.

What type of policies does SAS offer its employees? Nothing out of this world, in all honesty: most employees have their own offices instead of being open-plant, offices tastefully decorated, food and coffee at very low prices, sports facilities, crèches, free health centres and health insurance cover, that sort of thing.[22]

Fortunately, the trend seems to have extended, at least so we hear, to the large corporations of the western world. In business, as in armies, casualties are inevitable, but smaller companies, which depend much more on the qualities and abilities of their employees, must do as much as possible to minimise them.

This is because a casualty in a huge company is not the same as one in an SME (small and medium enterprise), just as a casualty in the Soviet army was not the same as one in the German army. The Russians possessed resources they could afford to squander, but the Germans did not.

Businesses are rather similar. Large corporations investing astronomical sums of money in R&D&I (Research, Development and Innovation), with immense cash flows, thousands of employees world wide, well-known and solvent brands, able to raise millions of dollars on the market for extra finance, and working in mature sectors, are like the Soviet Union Army. Smaller companies, however, in freshly developed markets, like the German Army, depend much more on their specialist and human teams.

Paradoxically, Human Resources are in much greater demand to minimise losses precisely where they are hardest to find. The first thought that comes into your head is that it is in a small company that there is neither time nor resources to consider minimising losses. Don't be surprised if you suddenly look around and find yourself all alone and in short sleeves before the gates of Moscow, in mid-winter with the Russian colossus waiting for you (map 3.3).

**Map 3.3 German advance into Russia
           (December 1941).**

So it turned out that November opened with the German troops half frozen, badly equipped, exhausted and decimated by months of endless fighting, yet still driven by the fact that Moscow and perhaps the end of the war were within reach.

However, despite the German efforts to continue to advance, the offensive ground to a halt at the beginning of December 1941. The German Army was exhausted and temperatures in the twenty degrees below zero prevented the tanks from moving easily. The logistics and supply system simply stopped working. Munitions and fuel failed to reach the forward troops as they usually did.

Apart from the deterioration of the weather conditions, December also witnessed the entrance of Japan in to the war. But the appearance of a new ally for the Axis contributed no special competitive advantage in itself because of the parallel war problem described before. Two of the best organised nations on earth (Germany and Japan), with the highest levels of education of their people, with powerful military traditions and extremely centralised decision making powers, were incapable of coordinating their forces, and decided to act in a completely independent fashion.

Japan attacked the USA, and the British (aware of how vitally important it was that the USA should join the Allied cause) declared war on Japan. Germany decided to declare war on the USA for no reason *[no casus belli]*, but Japan preferred to remain on the margin of the struggle in which its ally was involved and preferred not to declare war on the Soviet Union.

In addition to this, Stalin had another advantage. His intelligence service informed him with plenty of time that Japanese aircraft were to attack the Americans and leave the Soviets in peace. This meant that the Russians could mobilise their Siberian troops, based in Asia in preparation for the Japanese threat, and use them to build a front against the Germans at the most decisive moment. And the Siberian troops were not just any type of soldiers; they were experienced men and equipped specifically for winter combat.

And this was not all Stalin did. Continuing with his practice of delegation so that he could concentrate on what he did best, he appointed Georgi Konstantinovich Zhukov as commander-in-chief of the centre section, and placed the defence of Moscow in his hands.

Zhukov was an able, popular commander, decisive, well-organised, who paid close attention to detail and expected the utmost from his men. He was remembered by those who served with him as a tough-minded commander, who sacked officers who lacked sufficient will to win, and also as someone who had a clear grasp of operational realities and could remain calm under the most adverse circumstances.[23]

The Soviets threw their 58 divisions at the *Werhmacht* at precisely the moment when German resources could be stretched no further and were at the point of greatest weakness, waiting to be in a position to capture Moscow. What now? Would Hitler face the same destiny that

Napoleon in 1812? (Napoleon invaded Russia with around 650,000 men on June 24th 1812 and six months later, after conquering Moscow, he was driven from Russian territory along with the survivors, rather less than 10% of his men).

The Germans hesitated, taken by surprise. The bitter truth was that they had nothing left to throw at the Soviet whirlwind which was upon them. The icy winter had crippled their tanks, their aircraft could see nothing under such extreme conditions and the men, frozen to the marrow, could not even fire their rifles, since they jammed under such low temperatures.

Incapable of resistance, the Germans withdrew: Moscow had been saved. But the Soviets had merely won a battle; winning the war still lay far off in the future, and their success in no way implied that the German army had been destroyed. The Russians lacked the communications, reserves and transport they needed to continue to pursue the Germans, so there was no rout, with an easy victory at the end.

For their part, the Germans doggedly resisted, following the orders sent by Hitler from Berlin – "Never retreat". The infantry fought fiercely on, with initiative, courage and imagination, and the front was stabilised at the cost of enormous losses of men and materiel.

As Napoleon had once said, "in war, a great disaster always points to great culprits."[24] and Hitler set out to track down who it was. He sacked a number of commanders (including Guderian), whom he accused of not having been sufficiently keen on "defence to the bitter end". He also relieved the three commanders of the North, Centre and South Armies on "health grounds".

He then went on to dismiss the Commander-in-Chief of the army, Von Brauchitsch, a position which was taken over by Adolf Hitler himself. The *Führer* became directly responsible for tactical matters and general strategy, overloading himself ridiculously with work and taking on duties for which he was totally lacking in experience and training. The leader of the Nazi party, the German Head of State and the Prime Minister... all were now also the supreme Head of the Armed Forces and Commander-in-Chief of the Army.

Similar situations are more common than you might think, particularly in family firms (even those which have a multinational dimension). Faced with the most trivial setback, the founder takes on the duties of marketing director and even product manager. He wastes his time, his own money and even his health doing jobs which he could (and should) contract out to a better trained and experienced professional. Never mind how brilliant you are, you have to be able to delegate, the right way to react to setbacks is not by increasing the workload of the one person in whose hands the fate of the company lies.

Hitler thought that he was the only person who could inject the will to win into his armies, yet all that was achieved by this decision was to overload himself with work and lose perspective of the situation. The actual upshot was that he ceased to add value in the one place where he might have been of greatest use.

Even so, Soviet losses during the campaign were still frightful, and even the most optimistic estimates put manpower losses at around 3,100,000 killed or taken prisoner (some statistics set the figure as high as four or even six million). Equipment losses accounted for 20,500 tanks, 100,000 pieces of artillery and mortars and 18,000 aircraft.[25] But Moscow and Leningrad had been saved, and Stalin's regime, along with the Red Army, was still standing.

The Germans had advanced 750 miles (the same as the distance between the English Channel and Warsaw) along a 600 mile front. They had fought bravely against an enemy which was always superior in numbers, with more resources and in some cases better equipment. The cost had been 174,000 dead and 36,000 missing,[26] many of whom were valuable officers and specialists. They had also lost vast quantities of materiel. All these loses just for the partial achievement of one of the intended objectives. And for the first time since September 1939, they had been defeated.

4

The Stalingrad Epic

The situation facing Germany in January 1942 was certainly much worse than it had been a year earlier. The *Blitzkrieg* against the Soviet Union had failed, Great Britain was not alone anymore and the Americans had now joined the fray, so the Germans were involved in a long war, and on two fronts, the worst possible scenario.

But all was not lost. There was no doubt that the Soviet Union had suffered huge losses in men, equipment and territory, and the German army had not been annihilated as the French had been in 1812. The Americans were also still hesitating on the matter of making their strength felt in Europe (they first had to deal with the Asian front, where Japan was crushing everything that stood in its way).

The game was still undecided and victory would go to whoever made fewest mistakes and optimised their resources. A case study worthy of any business school class for the very topmost of executives would be this: What would you have done if you had had the chance of guiding Germany's fate in January 1942?

1. Summertime Blues

There is no doubt that the best chance of success for the Germans was to destroy the Russians, or at least cripple their ability to manoeuvre, so that when the Americans and British were ready for the re-conquest of Europe, the German army would have its hands free to face them with its military might. Yet again Germany confronted the dilemma: What should they do? And once again, Germany launched itself on a huge leap in the dark, betting everything on one card. Hitler opted for "Case Blue", which meant the conquest of Stalingrad (now Volgograd) and the Caucasus.

In theory it might be thought an acceptable plan. If successful, it would cut the main communications channel between the south and the rest of the country (the Volga river) and at the same time the Caucasus oil wells would be captured. It would seriously weaken the Soviets and would put an end to German problems regarding oil supplies, as well as closing the Black Sea ports to aid from the Allies. Stalingrad also had the added strategic value that it could serve as a base to launch an operation towards the Middle East and hence cut Allied supplies which were coming in through Iran; and Germany could even conquer India with the help of the Japanese.

As happens so often, it looked good on paper, but the reality was that Germany's resources were stretched to the limit in quest of an ever grander goal. Even if Case Blue turned out to be a success, the Russians would probably carry on fighting as would the Western Allies. The basic problem would not have been solved.

The *Werhmacht* High Command did not discuss strategic priority, partly because they, too, had no better alternative to recommend.[1] Germany lacked a coordinated command structure with critical capacity. The team was competing for the *Führer*'s approval, and the various power factions strove to make things even more absurd and radical as long as they were in the same direction as Hitler's thinking (or at least, what they thought might be the *Führer*'s ideas).

Events turned out better than could have been expected, when the German army annihilated a Russian offensive in the same zone in May. The balance sheet included 29 Soviet divisions destroyed, 200,000 men taken prisoner and 400 tanks destroyed.[2] Nor was this the only success, since other counter-attacks on other fronts, such as Leningrad, also ended up as Soviet losses. The enemy was becoming weaker.

Case Blue thus opened with excellent prospects. On June 28th 1942 the Soviets were taken by surprise, and once again the Panzers advanced purposefully over the Russian steppes, heading for the river Don and beyond, towards the Volga, and towards the borders of Europe.

On July 17th, with Stalingrad in reach, Hitler met with the head of the General Staff of his Armed Forces, General Franz Halder, and demanded: "Why not take Stalingrad and the Caucasus at the same time? Our men are tough enough to seize both objectives simultaneously."

Halder, the expert, was doubtful. He was for maintaining the concentration of forces at the point of maximum effort and keeping to the original plan (which included a first strike with the whole of the force at Stalingrad and falling on the Caucasus afterwards).

But Hitler now felt that victory was in his grasp and decided to impose his view, with another leap in the dark in quest of a miracle. "We shall do both things at the same time, the Russians are so weakened that they will be unable to stop us," he reasoned.

But not content with this, he thinned down the concentration of forces even more, sending five divisions to conquer Leningrad (pointlessly, since it was now too late, even if he had it in his grasp in 1941), plus two divisions of the German army elite (the *Leibstandarte* Adolf Hitler and *Grossdeutschland*, known as Germany's bodyguard) as reinforcements to France, where the British effort to launch an assault in the vicinity of Dieppe had collapsed in failure.

This loss of concentration and vision would have terrible consequences for the German army, doomed to capture none of the planned objectives. Remember – you shouldn't bite off more than you can chew...

In addition to this, the Soviets had now begun to get the measure of the German tactics. Learning from a string of defeats, they were beginning to realise that success when attacked by Panzer divisions was to be achieved by avoiding the pincer movements employed by the armoured forces. The best troops in the world were useless if they were surrounded and out of reach of their supply line. Their attitude also changed, shifting from the old idea of defending their land at all costs. This new strategy meant that troops were no longer sacrificed pointlessly and the much-desired collapse of the Russian army never happened.

Another step forward in countering the advance of the enemy was the realisation of the importance of synchronisation in the German attack. It was like a well-oiled machine which depended on all the parts moving in unison, and coordination between the various units in the action. Halting or slowing any of them affected all the others, slowing down all advances.

For example, establishing the front very close to the German positions made it very difficult for the *Luftwaffe* to operate, as it ran the risk of bombing its own troops. The defense in depth established by the Soviets as a response to the *Blitzkrieg* forced the various factions of the German army to halt then re-start over and over again when they attacked, thus avoiding the lightning progress of the *Werhmacht*. The advance was not stopped, but it was delayed, and its effectiveness decreased at the same time as a greater number of casualties were inflicted, since the front did not crumble so easily, and the Russians avoided being surrounded or routed as they had been in the previous year.

Nevertheless, at first things went reasonably well for the Germans, advances were significant, even despite huge supply problems, fierce resistance from the Soviets and the shortage of tanks. During July and August the Germans took around 625,000 prisoners, captured or destroyed 7,000 tanks, 6,000 pieces of artillery and 400 aircraft (considerable losses but not at the 1941 level). But this time the Germans suffered considerable casualties (nearly 200,000 in August alone, dead, wounded and missing).[3] By September 1942 the advance on the Caucasus had halted from sheer exhaustion (Map 4.1).

Meanwhile, further to the north, the Germans had reached Stalingrad. The importance of the enclave lay in its quality as an industrial city (with a population of nearly half a million), its river port and its important rail junction. Strategically it was a city which would be difficult to take because it would be impossible to surround, being strung out along the river Volga.

Map 4.1 German summer offensive of 1942.

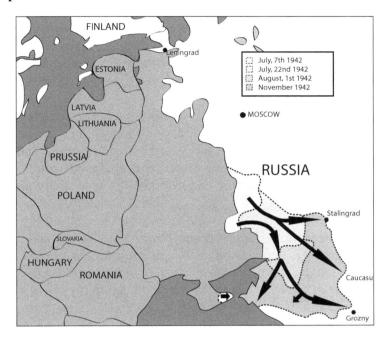

To make matters more complicated still for the German Army, the delay caused by the splitting and thinning down of the forces had given the Soviets sufficient time to garrison the city. Military logic thus recommended planning a flanking attack, with attempts to cross the river further to the south or the north, cutting river traffic and weakening the defence.

This was not the solution chosen. Like the bull in the ring, the Germans attacked the cape instead of taking the bullfighter from behind. Soon Stalingrad was to become a symbol (of resistance, as well as because of the importance of its name) and both Germans and Soviets threw everything they had into a battle for a goal no more important than so many others. As chess genius Gary Kasparov says in his book *How Life Imitates Chess: Making the Right Moves, from the Board to the Boardroom* "it is difficult to maintain your course and avoid the temptation of picking up the competitor's gauntlet and accepting the challenge. This demands very firm self-control, because the pressure to change is enormous. Our ego wants to prove that we can beat him on his own ground."

On September 15th a first mass attack was launched, with the foreseeable disastrous balance sheet of great losses and small advances. Plan B was deployed: large-scale bombing and fresh assaults, with the same outcome. This was when imagination ran out, and instead of seeking an alternative, they kept on with the widespread bombing of the city and more assaults.

It was the scenario of the First World War all over again: frontal assaults by the infantry against a well dug-in enemy, tiny advances and appalling casualties. Strangely, this was the kind of war that the German High Command, including Hitler, had promised would never happen again. Of course, they had said just the same thing about a war on two fronts.

The battle became a slaughterhouse, with both Hitler and Stalin hurling their men into the battle where they fought the foe until collapsing of exhaustion, a battle of attrition. It was what the Germans called a war of the rats. Advances were counted in metres, the dead and wounded (on both sides) in their thousands.

We should bear one of the strategic principles we defined in Chapter 1 in mind: manouvre. According to Liddell Hart, a breakthrough can be achieved in two ways, directly or indirectly.

- Direct approach to the enemy consisted of doing what the Germans had done at the gates of Stalingrad: a frontal assault using all the military weight available to achieve the desired breakthrough. The enemy can prepare for this relatively easily, fortifying his positions, which seriously compromises the chances of success. Indeed, military history shows that this type of manoeuvre usually fails, especially if the front is narrow and there is little leeway for movement. If it should happen that this move is successful it is usually at the price of a huge quantity of casualties and resources.

- The indirect approach consists of trying to guess what the enemy is expecting us to do, so that we can do the opposite. Unfortunately, in the military as well as the business world, the shortest distance between two points is almost always the furthest from victory. The goal is to find a breaking point which is both vital and vulnerable so that it can be destroyed with an economy of forces; to seek out the pivot, the Achilles heel that brings Goliath to the dust, regardless of his armour and his superiority over us in strength and height. This type of approach requires flexibility, mobility and surprise. Our opponent must be caused to lose his balance, to reveal his weak point, so that we can hit it as hard as possible. We must manoeuvre, let him show us his weaknesses, create new room on the chessboard.

At the end of the eighties of the twentieth century, the Japanese manufacturers of memory chips, launched a frontal attack on the multinational Intel. Their strategy was simple and direct: to undercut any price Intel could offer. Intel (Integrated Electronics) was already a multinational, despite its youth (it was founded in 1971), which specialised in making memory chips for computers and calculators.

Andrew Grove, CEO since 1987, decided to counter-attack using an indirect approach. An attempt to equal the low price made no sense, because he knew that in a battle to slash margins, the Japanese had the winning hand, so he attacked where the competitors least expected, where they were weakest. Firstly, he concentrated his forces at the point of maximum effort. From then on Intel would specialise in microprocessors (memory chips with the power to process data), which until then had been merely a niche business.

To increase margins, Intel decided to market its microhips directly to end consumers (previously, they had only regarded computer-makers as their only customers). The campaign *Intel Inside*, awarded the company with an unheard-of awareness for a manufacturer of this type of technology. Nobody had considered doing anything like this... until then.

Intel launched itself to the mass market like any other advertiser, and the label *Intel Inside* (stuck on any device which uses its microchips) became a brand recognisable by the final consumer, rendering the company immune to the price war and adding great value to Intel technology.[4]

The indirect strategy was a success, and from them on Intel has been the absolute leader at world level in the manufacture of microprocessors, with a market share greater than all its rivals put together (according to its own website, its market share in September 2009 was 80% at global level).

However, we should return to September 1942. With a lack of progress dominating the situation, as in the previous winter, the generals began to be fired. Wilhelm List, marshal of the Army Group entrusted with the capture of the Caucasus was relieved of his command and his position taken over by the Supreme Commander of the Armed Forces, Commander-in-Chief of Army, Head of Government, Leader of the National Socialist party and President of Germany[5]: Adolf Hitler.

Naturally, Hitler's assumption of command solved none of the supply problems nor the fact that neither of the two forces was strong enough by itself to capture either of the two objectives. Franz Halder, Head of the General Staff, was sacked on September 24th and another general was appointed to the position who was more convinced than his predecessor of the advantages of working in line with the *Führer*'s intention.

Adding yet more to the workload of the already pressured Hitler and his already swamped ability brought absolutely nothing to the German side, nor did the dismissal of Halder, an expert collaborator and his replacement by Kurt Zeiztler, another expert, but one with a much less critical approach.

Whatever the situation was in reality, now that he was less encumbered by criticism, the *Führer* continued to lean hard on Stalin and after two months of bloody struggle, on November 12th 1942, the final German attack was launched. Apart from a mere few square metres, Stalingrad was in the hands of the *Werhmacht*. The situation did not greatly disturb the Soviets. For two months now Stalin had been playing a different game, and very soon whoever was master of the city was to be a matter of no importance whatsoever.

2. Uranus: Zhukov's Trap

While Hitler was busy getting rid of his generals because of their lack of progress in the Caucasus, and was even trying to use his tanks in an absurd house-by-house battle in Stalingrad, the Russians were planning their revenge: operation Uranus.

Since mid-September the Soviet strategy had changed and the obsession to hold the city at all costs had been rethought. This was because the direct approach to the defence of the city had achieved no identifiable success and left behind a mountain of corpses. The game had to change; Stalingrad would be defended with the minimum number of men needed to actually keep the defence on its feet.

However, at the same time, new armies were massing behind the lines, bent on a grand encirclement operation.[6] The idea was not to actually surround the city itself, or even to relieve the pressure, but in reality a much more ambitious plan was afoot. The strategy, which could be seen as simple and to some degree obvious, was not to attack the Germans where they were strongest, the direct approach, but to seek out their weak point, even though this involved a more serious logistical problem.

The weak link was none other than the German's allies: Romanians, Hungarians and Italians, who were garrisoning sectors hundreds of kilometres from the point of maximum effort being sustained by what was known as the Sixth Army (that entrusted with the capture of Stalingrad).

Large reserves of men and materiel were mustered. On the one hand the USSR, the Soviet Union, had four times the tank manufacturing capacity of the German industry and in addition was being supported by British and American aid in the supply of lorries, vehicles, food and equipment. And on the other, despite what Hitler was expecting, its human resources were a long way from running out.

The risk of some flanks being over-exposed for the Germans was to some extent predictable, but together with the lack of significant advances, the danger had increased to levels of unsustainable fool-hardiness.

Field-marshal Friedrich Paulus was Commander-in-Chief of the Sixth Army. Paulus was a seasoned expert, conscientious and meticulous, but who afforded somewhat excessive importance to the chain of command. Obsessed with his work, he loved to devote his nights to the study of maps, a coffee in one hand and a cigarette in the other. He was often described as "more of a scientist than a general."[7]

While powerful Soviet forces were massing on the flanks of the Sixth Army, Paulus, sensing the danger, decided to do nothing more than send his reports to the *Führer*'s headquarters. This passive attitude was contrary to Prussian military tradition, which saw inactivity (merely awaiting orders) as an unforgivable mistake in a commander.[8] The example has an interesting application in business. We often act like Paulus facing the Soviet threat. "I've already told my boss that this is urgent, but I'm doing nothing until he tells me what to do."

At five am in the frigid dawn of November 19th, the regiments of mortars, artillery and mobile rocket launchers (mounted on lorries), the mythical Katyushas, received the order to open fire on the doomed Romanians. Operation Uranus had begun.

Waves of Russian infantry and combat tanks hurled themselves onto the Romanian lines, which held for a while. But by the end of the morning the defences were crippled and the Soviet tanks were racing towards Kalach, a small town on the banks of the river Don (and only 50 miles from Stalingrad).

Paulus received the first news of the Russian attack at about ten in the morning. His first reaction was to support the Romanians, although without much conviction. The weather was horrific and the as yet still powerful *Luftwaffe* lay in its airfields, unable to take off. By midnight Paulus was still uncertain of the Soviet intentions. His orders were unclear because he was still awaiting a reply from Berlin as to what to do, a reply which failed to appear.

Where was the *Führer*? As luck would have it, on the nineteenth he was travelling in Bavaria. The concentration of power in Hitler's person meant that without his physical presence, the control of the *Werhmacht* was paralysed. Worse still, when he heard the news, he gave express orders that nothing was to be done until he reached headquarters.

The Russians attacked again on the morning of the 20th. The objective this time was the south of Stalingrad where they were once again opposed by the Romanians, who, as on the previous day, were shattered and withdrew in great confusion. This was the second wing of the Soviet pincer which was about to attempt to crush the German Sixth Army.

An initial counter-attack, light on men and means, achieved almost nothing. Hitler, kept informed at all times, hesitated and allowed himself to be swayed by his fear of withdrawal. Perhaps there was actually nothing to be done, but he gave no order: it had cost too much to take on Stalingrad and reach the Volga to abandon it just like that.

On the following day (November 21th) the Soviet northern wing reached Kalach. The situation became more complicated by the moment. An anxious Paulus was still unsure, although Soviet intentions became more obvious by the minute (Map 4.2).

Map 4.2 Soviet attack against the Sixth German Army

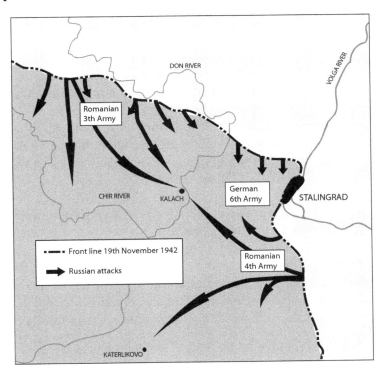

3. The Wise Man makes Corrections while the Fool remains in Error

On the night of November 22th 1942, the *Führer* at last reached his headquarters. He informed Paulus that he would take a decision on the following day, so that until he received fresh instructions he was to hold his position and not give an inch. The news on the following day was not encouraging for the Germans: the two jaws of the Soviet vice had met up very near Kalach. Paulus and all his Sixth Army, together with some Croatian and Romanian units, plus some of the *Luftwaffe* (in total, some 250,000 men), was enclosed in a huge pocket.[9]

But the troops within the noose knew that there was still a chance, that the Sixth Army could still break out by catching the Russians while they were still in motion, still off guard, and make it very difficult for them to maintain the siege. This counter-offensive would make it possible to open a gap through which the troops could be evacuated. This strategy would imply losing Stalingrad but would mean there was a chance of a response which would inflict serious damage on the Russians.

Meanwhile, back at the Wolf's Lair, Hitler and his General Staff were meeting, analysing the situation and trying to decide whether to withdraw or to resist and try to break the encirclement from outside. Just for a moment, faced with the enormity of the military situation, Hitler toyed with the idea of allowing the withdrawal (which was what all his commanders in the zone were pleading for). It was the moment to consult his faithful advisors.

Herman Goering was decisive: "Sir, the fortress of Stalingrad can be supplied from the air by my *Luftwaffe*. We shall turn Stalingrad into another Toledo Alcazar![10]" His words were grabbed out of the air, based on no analysis of the situation and backed by no reliable data or realistic calculations. He had allowed himself to be carried away by excitement, taking no account of the fact that the forces of the Red Army had very little to do with the Spanish republican militia.

- "I shall never give up the Volga", Hitler then declared.

- "No, sir. We shall never give up the Volga", chorused Wilhelm Keitel, German Chief of Armed Forces since 1940 (a position he had earned thanks to his blind faith and lack of critical faculties).

- "The decision we must take is really serious, sir... let's wait for the outcome of the operations as they proceed, and until we know how these operations will turn out, I believe we should continue to hold our position on the Volga"[11], agreed Alfred Jold, Chief of the Operation Staff of Armed Forces.

This support allowed Hitler to ignore any temptation to consider a withdrawal, and he clung to these arguments as grounds for his decision that the Sixth Army would resist until an offensive could release it.

This is what usually happens when we have surrounded ourselves with subordinates who have climbed the ladder solely thanks to their ability to work blindly in the direction pointed out by the leader, specialists in telling us precisely what we want to hear... which is why we so like listening to them. But their skill in always putting us in the right and their lack of a critical faculty may hide something worse: their total and absolute incompetence. This combination is a sure bet on a disaster of Stalingrad-size proportions.

At first light on the morning of November 24th the decision was communicated. The The Stalingrad fortress[12] was established on the premise that the Sixth Army would resist until reinforcement arrived. All the hopes of the commanders in the field were utterly dashed. At the same time a plan was drawn up to create a corridor, and General Von Manstein was appointed head of the group of armies which would carry out this mission.

The final days of November were full of anxiety for the besieged men. Goering's promises to supply the Sixth Army from the air proved to be utterly impractical and exaggerated and the lack of provisions weakened the troops further with every passing day.

In the meantime the Soviets were preparing their second blow, Operation Saturn, intended to protect the Stalingrad defences and anticipate a German counter-attack. Soviet forecasts were accurate as to the direction of the German attack, but the speed and violence of Von Manstein's counter-offensive shook them. A good leader, Manstein had not waited for optimum conditions and had taken the Russians by surprise. The date was December 12th. Six days later the German vanguards had penetrated into the Soviet defenses and are only 30 miles from Stalingrad. Would there be a miracle? Was the Sixth Army to be freed without having to abandon the Volga?

The answer was not slow in coming. They could advance no further. The Soviets unleashed a modified version of their Operation Saturn and struck the Italian Army which was protecting the northern flank of the Germans who were battling for the Volga. The Italians collapsed just as the Romanians had done a month before. The Russians had refused to play the German game, they had not directly opposed the armoured formations, and adopting an indirect approach, they rendered the German forces useless (since the Russians were now threatening the city of Rostov, and if they took it a million Germans would trapped between Stalingrad and the Caucasus, including Von Manstein himself).

The situation was now very dangerous for Manstein. He implicitly challenged Hitler, so he asked Paulus to prepare to abandon the siege and join him. He had little time left before he would have to make a speedy withdrawal in order to avoid being surrounded by the Russians himself.

With no explicit order from Hitler, Paulus hesitated and replied that it was impossible for him to join up with Manstein because his tanks barely had fuel enough to drive 20 miles. His own generals were insisting that he abandon his equipment and open the way to Manstein using the infantry as the only sure way out.[13]

The situation in which Paulus as an expert, a firm believer in procedures and the chain of command, found himself was itself far from easy. He could choose between taking on fewer risks and remaining within the fortress, the easier decision, but one which would seal his fate and that of his men, or take the operational risk of breaking out, knowing that Hitler would not like it, but it might save his men… Paulus decided to do nothing. Manstein withdrew and the German troops in Stalingrad were abandoned to their fate.

In our everyday working lives, and in our personal lives, too, we have to take decisions continually, decisions which mean risks. Taking risks and sacrificing today for tomorrow can be frightening. So making no choice is preffered to risking the blame for a bad choice.[14] Like Paulus at the end of December 1942 we have to work out whether our aversion to risk is based on an objective analysis of the situation or merely an apparent convenience if we wish to know whether the decision will leave us in the same situation as the German soldiers in Stalingrad.

Despite leaving a huge breach in the German machine, Manstein managed to buttress the front after the collapse of the Italians while still keeping the corridor which allowed the Army of the Caucasus to retreat in good order. However Stalingrad was now 140 miles from the German lines.

To make matters worse, the Soviets now attacked the Second Hungarian Army, destroying it and opening a 200 mile hole in the German lines. There was no possibility of lifting the siege of Stalingrad.

On February 2nd 1943, the last German troops surrendered and handed over the Stalingrad fortress (in all, 91,000 men were taken prisoner). Military losses were the equivalent of six months-worth of production of armour and vehicles, four months-worth of artillery production and several more additional months-worth of small arms.[15]

It was the greatest collapse of German arms since the beginning of the war, but it would not be the last nor the most serious. The German machine in southern Russia was now in grave danger. Perhaps, after all, 1943 would see the end of the war.

5

Back at *Mare Nostrum*

1. The Maltese Falcon

While the *Werhmacht* was losing strength throughout the length and breadth of the Soviet Union, what had happened to our innovator Rommel and his Afrika Korps? We should recall that on the eve of the invasion of the USSR we had left the British on the point of aiming a mortal blow at the Afrika Korps and their Italian allies: operation Battleaxe.

However, in spite of material and manpower superiorities, the British had crashed against the German lines and had suffered a serious defeat and numerous losses. The upshot of this disaster was that the allied General Staff had decided to replace Archibald Wavell with Claude Auchinleck as British Commander-in-Chief of the Middle East with the clear objective of destroying the Afrika Korps once and for all. For the British it was most important that the Germans be driven out of North Africa as soon as possible to avoid the possibility that a German victory in Russia would allow Hitler to send his Panzers across the Caucasus heading for the Persian Gulf.

This haste was one of the main reasons for the change of leadership of the troops. In reality this decision is not unlike a situation in business when the management loses confidence in its CEO.

Past successes mean little – he has to go. So Wavell was "promoted" to Viceroy of India and replaced by Auchinleck, who was reinforced with more tanks, aircraft and supplies, no insignificant factor given the importance of logistics, a crucial factor in the war in North Africa and the very point where the combatants were making their greatest efforts.

This scenario became a kind of competition arena in which each army rushed forward in turn until they were almost exhausted. The armies advanced and withdrew to where they had come from to avoid annihilation. The basic reason for this was directly connected with supplied. Like a piece of elastic, the communication lines of both armies could be stretched with relative safety up to between 300 and 400 miles between their bases (Tripoli for the Germans and Alexandria for the British).

The distance between both bases (1,400 miles) meant that it was impossible to draw out the lines of communication without previously having set up intermediate bases, and the attempt to do so meant risking breaking them completely. The supply problem lay (for both sides) in their ability to increase the elasticity of their respective systems. This meant that it was vital to accumulate stores at the home bases and then move them step by step to the advance bases. The distance between both combatants and their respective mother countries meant that sea communications became vital.[1]

In this battle for supplies the British depended on two important bases: Gibraltar, and above all, Malta (the importance of this island lay in its position in the middle of the Axis communication lines, which meant that it was a perfect base for attacking supplies being moved from Italy to North Africa).

The Italians had let the opportunity to take Malta in June 1940 slip between their fingers – at that time the island was protected only by three ancient aircraft (christened, not without some degree of irony, Faith, Hope and Charity). But that had not been the only chance, since in the spring of 1941 the Germans and Italians could have taken it quite easily, and certainly at less cost and greater gains than Crete. But they had contented themselves by damping its offensive power by bombing. In the autumn of 1941, with the bulk of the *Luftwaffe* in the Russian steppes, the British made the most of the situation to transform it into a lethal base from which submarines and aircraft inflicted great losses on Italian and German supplies.

Hence, on November 18th 1941, with Malta like a nightmare and Tobruk at their back, Rommel's position was somewhat borderline when the British operation Crusader, their fourth offensive in North Africa, was launched.

British superiority in terms of tank numbers and air support was fielded by Rommel by means of a series of rapid feints which disconcerted his enemy, so the outcome for some days was uncertain. "The Desert Fox" had fewer resources but concentrated them more effectively.

Auchinleck was tempted by some of his staff to abandon the project, since there was a risk of losing everything and gaining nothing. But the commander did not hesitate, and decided to stand firm. He accepted the risk and calculated that the enemy was in a worse position than he was… Indeed, Rommel abandoned the game and withdrew.

On November 25th Tobruk was liberated after a siege of nearly seven months. Now that the German lines were broken, the British continued their advance and although they failed to trap Rommel, on January 11 1942 they re-conquered the Cyrenaic peninsula for the second time. The German withdrawal in Libya occurred at the same time as the *Werhmacht* was in strife in Moscow. After two years of warfare, the British had for the first time defeated German forces on the ground. And although for the first time there was a real possibility of driving the Germans and Italians from north Africa, the reality was that it was the British who had stretched their lines of communication too far. Now it was the turn of the Italian/Germans to start playing like locals.

In addition, the Germans had send 25 submarines from the Atlantic and a *Luftwaffe* air corps from the Soviet Union front (which took some of the pressure off both British and Soviets, in the battles of the Atlantic and Moscow respectively). The consequences of these movements were almost instantaneous and during January 1942 the Axis lost not a single ton of equipment on the Mediterranean crossing.[2]

Malta was shut down once again by violent bombing and this time real damage was done. And in the meantime the British lost an aircraft-carrier, three battleships and two cruisers, which meant that the allied air/sea power was the weakest it had been since the start of the war.

Under these changed circumstances, Rommel, who never found it easy to remain inactive, and who was seldom daunted by failures, ordered the counter-attack barely ten days after the conclusion of the British offensive (at the end of January 1942).

Rommel had outlined a strategy intended to avoid the errors of his previous campaign: the first objective was to take Tobruk and from there the whole of Libya. Point two was an assault on the island of Malta, and when that was in his hands, he would launch an offensive to occupy Egypt. During April and May the British had been fiercely defending the length of the Cyrenaic peninsula. Auchinleck withdrew slowly as the lesser evil to avoid being surrounded by Rommel. While this was taking place an intense bombing campaign was being waged against Malta to weaken its defences and streamline the progress of Operation Hercules (intended to capture Malta by sea).

At the same time, just when the British were preparing a new counter-attack with Tobruk as their base, Rommel threw himself at the southern flank of the British, from the desert, and swinging northwards took Tobruk by assault, capturing 33,000 prisoners and a huge amount of military supplies (Map 5.1).

The fall of Tobruk was an immense shock for the allies, and stood as the last stroke of a series of disasters for the British, which Churchill called "a sombre pause".[3] But as they had in the glorious isolation of 1940, the British resisted without complaint or hesitation, and also without failing.

Despite the setbacks, the British Parliament (the equivalent of the shareholders' meeting in the business world) endorsed Churchill in his position. The people showed clear support for the head manager, a byword for motivation and commitment in the face of adversities and losses. Churchill was equal to the task and managed to persuade the Americans to come to the aid of the British army by sending 300 tanks and 100 self-propelled guns to Egypt, despite their own urgent requirements.

Map 5.1 Libya and Egypt (1942-1943).

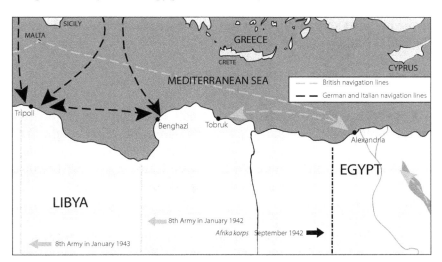

A witness eloquently described the reaction aroused by the message sent by the British and American leaders: "Tobruk, in the African desert, had just fallen to the Germans, and the whole allied world was thrown into gloom. But these two leaders (Churchill and Roosevelt) showed no signs of pessimism. It was gratifying to note they were thinking of attack and victory, not defence and defeat."[4]

What is certain is that, although 1941 had ended badly for the Germans (after the defeats in Moscow and Libya), the summer of 1942 had changed the course of the war: the *Wehrmacht* was advancing victoriously towards Egypt and towards the limits of the steppes in the USSR. Had the Allied victories in 1941 been an illusion? Neither Churchill nor Stalin felt that this was the case.

In the African desert, as previously in their advance on Stalingrad and the Caucasus, the Germans once again lost their vision. Encouraged by Rommel's remarkable success in Tobruk, they decided to throw away the route map they had drawn up beforehand and to advance on Egypt, ignoring the danger implied in this venture if Malta had not been crushed. "The Desert Fox", with Hitler's blessing, made a bad decision (great leaders, experts or innovators, all make mistakes – none is infallible).

Having lost Tobruk, the British were betting on El Alamein, the last line of defence before the River Nile. Now the British were playing at home and had shorter supply lines. But not even that factor daunted the battle-hardened Afrika Korps.

2. El Alamein

The importance of El Alamein, a small rise close to the coastal fringe, was that some 35 miles towards the south, in a straight line, lay the Qattara depression, swampy and impassable by heavy armies. Surrounding it at the southern edge was all but impossible because it would demand a huge amount of equipment and supplies, which both sides lacked.

Entry into Egypt would force Rommel to pass through this bottleneck between the sea and the Qattara depression. This area was scattered from east to west by a series of small elevations, never higher than 300 metres, but which in that flat terrain were formidable obstacles.[5]

The British dug in there, building four defense in depth positions which would protect, behind the last line, the only freshwater springs in the zone. For a few days in July it appeared that the Axis troops would be able to enter Alexandria with ease, and in fact the British had made plans for a second line of defence on the Nile, in Palestine and even in Iraq.

But Rommel's lucky star was on the wane, and after a brilliant 400-mile dash at the end of May, the Afrika Korps troops were exhausted, almost out of supplies, and surviving on what they had captured from the British during the advance. When they reached El Alamein, the situation was so precarious that the Germans possessed no more than thirteen tanks.[6] Rommel was forced to come to a halt to regroup and seek provisions if he wished to deploy any offensive capability.

The British, knowing what was at stake, raised the ante and made a supreme effort to reactivate Malta as an offensive base. Although causing important British naval losses, the island was re-armed yet again to provide it with air and sea capacity sufficient to strangle the Afrika Korps.

Once they had achieved this, a powerful air offensive was launched to cut the supply route between Italy and Africa. The *Luftwaffe* strove to prevent this for some time, but the Russian front was consuming almost all its resources in both aircraft and men, and the defence was feeble.

At the same time British factories, and at an increasingly overwhelming rate, American industries, were supplying huge quantities of materiel to their troops in Egypt. With every passing day the British grew stronger and the Italians and Germans weaker.

Even so, despite the somewhat desperate position in which the Germans found themselves, they were still able to stabilise the front at the end of July. Winston Churchill arrived on a visit to Cairo in August with the firm proposition of driving the Germans out of North Africa once and for all.

As often happens in business, Churchill decided that in order to tackle the fresh challenge, apart from providing the necessary resources, it was absolutely essential that a gesture be made by the person at the very top of the organisation. He therefore appointed Bernard "Monty" Montgomery Commander-in-Chief of the Eighth Army (the British troops posted to the African desert).

The relief of Auchinleck was intended to act as a spur, to instil a new feeling and draw a line under the Tobruk disaster. A new general was needed with a reputation which had not yet been tarnished by the myth of the Desert Fox. Of importance in making this decision were Auchinleck's poor communication skills and his ability to irritate Churchill (firstly because he preferred to withdraw in order to keep his force intact, and secondly because he was more concerned with beating Rommel than attending to the Prime Minister's requirements).[7]

In real life we often witness this: a good manager is replaced by another who is not so good but who ends up with all the honours thanks to the good work of his predecessor. This may be unfair, but it happens if this is what the business needs. When it does happen, the best thing is not to take it badly, particularly if you have worked well and been decently loyal to the organisation. Arbitrary it may be, but it happens every day.

Montgomery was every inch an expert: calculating, cautious, disciplined, organised, pragmatic and an astute master of public relations. He was also imbued with great determination and self-confidence. And what is certain is that by training and discipline he managed to instil in the Eighth Army the spirit of victory.

Aware of Rommel's upper hand in a mobile war, he decided to shift the battle onto his own ground, accumulating his reserves and patiently waiting for the moment when he would be in a much better position. Yielding the initiative to Rommel was an implicit acknowledgement of his superior skill and his innovation, but he dared not risk another defeat, however much London might urge him to produce a result as quickly as possible.

The right thing for him to do was to be patient and avoid a face-off in a game where he knew his opponent was superior, so he decided to create his own scenario. In this respect he had a number of factors in his favour which his predecessors lacked. In the first place, geography was forcing Rommel to attack in a bottleneck. Secondly, The Germans were on the brink of exhaustion in Stalingrad while Monty's troops were benefiting from American industrial potential. As Napoleon put it, "I prefer a lucky general to a good general."

But lucky or not, it cannot be denied that *Monty* faced his challenges and emerged victorious. Retaining market share for a company like Coca-Cola is of course easier than launching yourself into a new entrepreneurial adventure in an emerging market, but that in no way means that managing Coca-Cola is easy, never mind the resources it possesses.

And in actual fact, at the beginning of the 1980's, Coca-Cola was indeed experiencing problems in the US and its market share was steadily sliding in favour of its rival Pepsi. Roberto Goizueta, an executive whose entire career had been with the soft drink multinational, was appointed CEO to change the situation. His first moves were very much those of the expert: he concentrated resources, eliminated unprofitable business lines, gave battle at the points of sale and in the minds of the customers.

Even so, and despite the fact that Coca-Cola spent 100 million dollars more then Pepsi per year on marketing, had more points of sale and offered better prices and discounts, the situation did not improve.

Millions of dollars were spent on market research. Why did the consumers prefer Pepsi? Then, somebody came up with a possible answer. In blind tests of the product, the consumers seemed to prefer the sweeter taste of Pepsi.

Having tried the ideas the expert comes up with, Goizueta now went the way of the innovator (based on devastating logic). The Coca-Cola formula had remained unchanged throughout the whole of the past century; it was to be changed to launch a new version, known as New Coke. The consumer would like the taste, more like that of Pepsi, and thus Coca-Cola would regain the initiative.

In 1985, the launch was supported with all the heavy artillery possessed by Coca-Cola. A massive advertising and public relations campaign was orchestrated *by land, sea and air*. 80% of the population of the USA was reached by the New Coke advertising in the first 24 hours of the campaign.

The distribution channels were also filled with product stocks, so that at any point in the United States, any customer would be able to buy the product after seeing the ad. The battle was on and, at least on paper, Coca-Cola held the winning hand... And indeed, people did rush to try New Coke.

But it didn't work out the way it should have. Traditional Coca-Cola began to run out in the shops and supermarket shelves, while an astronomical number of complaints were received throughout the length and breadth of the country about the flavour of New Coke. After ten weeks the company was forced to retract and re-launch traditional Coca-Cola under the name Coca-Cola Classic.

How could this be possible if all the decisions had been made on the basis of intelligent research backed by vast quantities of data? It was simply that they had misinterpreted the information they had gleaned about the consumer, an error of methodology and perception. Customers were not looking for a sweeter Coca-Cola – they liked the taste of Pepsi, but they had an emotional commitment to Coca-Cola, the value of a century of work.

By the end of 1985 Pepsi had overtaken the Coca-Cola market share[8] and the managers of the brand in Atlanta were at their wits end. And yet, the strange thing is that in 1986 they became market leaders once again, thanks to an upturn in the sales of (unbelievable) Coca-Cola Classic!

But let us return to the sands of the desert in August 1942. Despite the promises he was receiving from Berlin, Rommel knew that his superiority over the British in terms of equipment was now a fantasy, and he decided to try a desperate move with the scanty resources available to him: he would launch an attack.

Monty was ready for the move and avoided the trap, allowing the German to squander his dwindling forces. Rommel achieved nothing, and was now even weaker. Montgomery, master of public relations, became overnight "the man who defeated the Desert Fox".

Rommel fell ill and went back to Germany for treatment, confident that he would be back in command of his men when the British decided to mop up the remains of the Afrika Korps.

On October 23rd Montgomery was prepared, and launched Operation Lightfoot, the philosophy of which was based on the military aphorism "hide what you have and show off what you lack". He feinted to the south and attacked to the north via a breach he had opened for the purpose in the German defences.

Aware of the gravity of the attacks the Desert Fox discharged himself from hospital and on October 25th was once again at the head of his men. With Rommel in place, the Germans did not allow themselves to be tricked and they constrained the expected breakthrough. The

British lost large numbers of tanks and failed in their attempt at a decisive victory.

Montgomery was undaunted by the setback. He remained calm, sure of himself, resisting pressure from Churchill, confident that the German effort to restrain him at the end of October would have mortally weakened the German army. Time was on his side.

On November 2nd, he launched his new offensive, Supercharge, changing the direction of the advance towards the south, in an attempt to drive a wedge between the German and Italian troops. Rommel resisted grimly and his situation became desperate. He was almost out of fuel for the vehicles, and was very short of tanks, aircraft and guns.

Two days later, defying Hitler himself, Rommel decided to withdraw, his troops now in a very precarious state. The only doubt was whether they would be surrounded and destroyed as had happened with Paulus's men in Stalingrad. But Monty was no Zhukov. Montgomery was much more cautious, much more concerned for the lives of his men which he was unwilling to risk unless he was sure the battle would be cost-efficient in terms of losses. Rommel was not annihilated, but within 20 days his men withdrew for the third time in two years from the Cyrenaic peninsula.

Although El Alamein was a limited victory, its importance to the Allies, and particularly for the British who had been at war since 1939, was immense; it was a turning point and a very important morale booster. As Churchill put it, "before El Alamein we never had a victory, and after it we never had a defeat."[9] In the headquarters in Berlin and Rome it might have been thought possible to stabilise the troops behind the Cyrenaic peninsula and once again establish a line of defence before Tripoli was reached. But this time it would be impossible. The Americans have come to change everything.

3. Tunisia: I think this is the beginning of a beautiful friendship

The Japanese attack on December 7th 1941 on Pearl Harbor (see Chapter 10) and an error of calculation on the part of the German management had brought the United States into the war against Germany, Italy and Japan. Churchill sensed that the involvement of the American variable unbalanced the equation in favour of the Allies,[10] but the fact was that between December 1941 and November 1942 the British and the Soviets had reaped nothing but failure.

Just being stronger is not enough, nor is having a good team, a good product, good finance and a great market opportunity. You have to be all those things at the point of maximum effort, and at the decisive moment. Market domination depends not just on the potential of a company, but on its ability to translate that to the point of sale, the supermarket shelf, to the customer's mind, and to tackle (and overwhelm) the competitor at the moment of purchase.

In February 1998, two of the largest and most powerful companies in Spain, Tabacalera and Cortefiel, leaders in their sectors, with vast experience, sound management teams and huge economic resources, launched the company known as Via Plus. The idea was simple, they would set up ATM-type points-of-sale, mostly in tobacconists, where people could choose from a wide range of products (books, CDs, computers, fashion clothes, etc.) at competitive prices. There were a total of 40,000 products, from over 150 brands.

In November 1999, Via Plus initiated its Internet sales activities. Despite the huge investment of financial and human resources and the support of important experts, the idea did not suceed at all. Three years and eighty million wasted Euros later, the business had to close.[11] So just being strong is not enough.

Would the entry of the United States into the war be a decisive factor in the conflict? Would they be able to position their superior resources at the decisive moment when faced with a determined competitor?

The day that Adolf Hitler invaded Poland, the entire armed forces of the United States was barely 300,000 strong. Six years later, in 1945, they had 12 million men in uniform, over 70,000 warships and nearly 73,000 aircraft.[12] What buttons had been pressed to make this possible?

The secret most definitely lay in two fairly simple recipes. The first was the ability to change the direction of a huge economy based on mass consumption swiftly and efficiently to focus it on the military effort (we shall examine this point in detail in the next chapter).

The second was the makeup of the military leadership: simple men, hard workers, good experts for whom human resources (that is, the lives of their men) were a valuable asset. It may be that none was a great military innovator or strategic genius of the calibre of Alexander the Great, Julius Caesar or Napoleon, and perhaps they even lacked the military experience of Guderian, Rommel or Von Manstein. But even so, they knew how to make the most of their resources and how to win a war without discarding their moral principles and keeping the losses of their compatriots to a minimum.

The main person responsible for this was their CEO, president Franklin Delano Roosevelt. His greatest skill was his ability to surround himself with skilled and effective team members, who allowed the generals to do their job without becoming bogged down in technical matters they understood nothing about. Their system operated with the minimum of friction and the maximum of effectiveness.

Roosevelt gave up the power granted him by the American Constitution which provides that as of the moment of his election, the president becomes supreme leader of the armed forces. United States history can provide numerous examples of greater involvement from the past, such as when Abraham Lincoln directed operations, not always successfully, during the American Civil War (1861 to 1865).

Roosevelt was not entirely ignorant of matters military, and thanks to his time as under-secretary of the army during the First World War, he was familiar in broad terms with problems of Strategy. Nevertheless, he preferred never to make use of this fact to put his personal stamp on operations[13] as his peers did (Churchill, Stalin, Mussolini and Hitler).

The US president understood his fellow-countrymen and the mechanism which drove his society. This allowed him to present an idealistic perception of the conflict, communicating to the citizens the vision of a new world order, one which was fairer and more free after the war. He succeeded in uniting the people's will and effort so that the diversity which characterised US society was converted into unity of action, with everybody supporting the struggle. Outstanding of his many virtues was the ability to appoint skilled people and to communicate confidence and optimism. He supplied inspiration, he remained steadfast, unruffed even by defeats, supportive to all round him. He kept his anxieties to himself, just as he kept his disability from the public gaze. He had the strength to recognise his limitations, in itself a hallmark of intelligent leadership.[14]

This is reminiscent of the time when the CEO of one of the main Spanish banks once told me that "as time passes I have come to realise that I really don't know much about anything, but what I do know is how to pick the people who do."

On the debit side, note should perhaps be made of his diffuse leadership style (which resulted sometimes in his team members being uncertain as to what policy to follow, and which sometimes led to his subordinates seeming to receive apparently contradictory instructions). He also had no strategic vision of the steps to take once Germany and Japan had been defeated.

One example would be the fact that he thought it would be possible to maintain cordial relations with Stalin, even at a personal level. He seemed to place too much faith in the power of his personal charm and charisma to influence people, and he often trusted too much in his ability to establish deep and lasting personal relationships. In this respect it should be borne in mind that Stalin also managed to deceive even Churchill. While Roosevelt said of the Soviet leader, "I can handle him", Churchill was hardly less effusive, declaring "I can do business with him". History would show how mistaken they both were.[15] Their incorrect calculations would leave half of Europe in the hands of a tyrannical, cruel and despotic government for 40 years after the World War, although this matter lies outside the scope of this book.

Great businessmen do indeed exist who have built business empires on the foundation of their personal charm. This is a tremendous ability, but everything they build is in danger of going down the drain if they lose their perspective and forget the existence of thousands

104

of Stalins with no feelings or scruples, acting as though they have been won over while they set their traps to catch their prey. In any case, this is but a small blot on his presidential escutcheon (unless you happen to be Polish, German, Lithuanian, Estonian, Latvian, Romanian, Hungarian, Czech, Slovakian, Serbian, Croat, Slovenian, Albanian, Bulgarian, Japanese or Korean).

Despite the fact that there were 33 generals with greater seniority, Roosevelt chose George Marshall as head of the General Staff of the armed forces. He was won over by his sincerity and the fact that he felt he could trust him. His intuition turned out to be right, since afterwards he became the "organiser of the Allied victory" (in the words of Winston Churchill himself).

Indeed, a business manager can learn a great deal from a man like Marshall. First and foremost was his ability to delegate so that he could then devote himself to what was really important "a coordinated programme and a single head", avoiding bureaucracy and allowing time for the key players to think about the fundamental problems. Those of us who have worked for a number of bosses know that delegation is the secret of leadership. Delegation means motivating others to do more than we can expect from ourselves. By delegation, we lead, and thus we inspire people. It is "mobilising within ourselves and in others what is most worthy in all of us, helping others to achieve a level greater than they expected, a level we knew was within their reach, even though they were unsure."[16]

Delegating means counting on your subordinates, and this is no easy decision (and certainly not automatic). It takes courage, trust and decisiveness. And it doesn't mean handing the hardest work or the complications to whoever is lowest in the food chain in the hope that he (or she) will find a solution. Delegation means ensuring that each level accepts the responsibility which is appropriate to it. As Mario Alonso Puig says in one of his books, "the greatest misfortune for the human being is failing to meet someone who helps you to discover what you could really be."[17]

Other aspects of George Marshall's management style are neatly described in the memoirs of an American general who was Marshall's comrade (Dwight D. Eisenhower, whom we shall meet later on):

- He was not fond of recommendations: "If he's your friend, the best thing you can do is not mention his name", he would say.

- He encouraged independence and asked his assistants to think and operate on their own account within their specialist field.

- He loathed people who insisted on seeing to minute details personally.

- He did not like people who confused firmness and gusto with bad manners, nor those who fell out with people, or who thrust themselves forward.

- He could never abide chronic pessimists who always saw the negative side of things, always assuming resources were insufficient.

- He never appointed an officer unless he was enthusiastic about a project and convinced of its ultimate success.

His attitude to the war was more that of a manager of a big corporation than of a general at war. He applied technocratic criteria to the job of building an army and choosing his strategy (for example, he streamlined the top of the army, reducing from 61 to six the number of officials with direct access to his office, and he divided the organisation into three major elements, army, air forces and supply). He devoted a great deal of his energy to training and logistics. In his opinion, war was a unified process from recruitment to combat.[18] This is surely reminiscent of Porter's value chain (the concept of the value chain is concerned with identifying the procedures and operations which add value to the business. It is about making ourselves strong where we add most value).[19]

His first good decision was that the strategic priority of the war lay in Europe and not Asia. This amounted to a decision taken in the teeth of the opinion of the American people, who were furious with the Japanese (and from whom they wanted revenge) but merely irritated with the Germans. It also contradicted the higher ranks of the Navy, who feared the overall superiority of the Japanese in the Pacific if action was not taken speedily.

In his opinion, however, it was essential to mass resources against Germany, since the risk of the collapse of the Soviet Union or Great

Britain before the USA could move the bulk of its resources to Europe (or of the Germans enjoying a prolonged rest), was much greater than the humiliating defeats the Japanese could inflict on them in the short term. He showed that he was capable of keeping his forces concentrated and not losing sight of the big picture when faced with events which were serious and disturbing but which did not change the strategic realities of the conflict.

The second realisation was that it was essential for the coalition of the Allies to remain strong and united in the face of setbacks. Unconcerned with theoretical positions, he insisted that the efforts of Great Britain and the United States should merge. For this purpose he appointed General Dwight Eisenhower, a man who worked on consensus, as supreme commander of the Allied forces in Europe.

Unlike the concept of parallel war adopted by the Axis powers, the Western Allies and the Soviet Union (particularly the first), strove to unite their diverse political, economic and military interests. In the end it was this coalition which was imposed, despite that fact that these three countries were made of "strong men representing strong and proud peoples".[20]

And if the relationship between Great Britain and the United States, notwithstanding good faith and the predisposition of their top leaders, needed a great deal of work, a great deal more was needed regarding the relationship between these two and the Soviet Union. But in spite of all the difficulties, the three nations remained united to the end, and did not yield until Germany, Italy and Japan had surrendered unconditionally. Their unity was their strength against the enemy.

Business is the same. According to a recent article in The Economist, at least 75% of mergers and takeovers fail and bring no profits for the shareholders for the very reason that unity is never achieved. And in actual fact, half of them lose value for the shareholders. Examples are legion: Quaker and Snapple, Daimler-Benz and Chrysler, Time Warner and AOL, etc.[21]

On November 8th, 1942, Operation Torch, led by Eisenhower, was launched. It basically consisted of landing an American contingent in Morocco and Algeria to advance swiftly on Tunisia with the aim of taking the Afrika Korps from behind and annihilating it as quickly as possible as a first step for a possible invasion of Italy.

Despite the fact that in theory it was assumed that the French colonial authorities would offer no resistance, they still had to be silenced by force of arms in order to be able to land in Morocco and Algeria (and although the picture does not match the literature which represents the majority of the French as heroes of the resistance, it is beyond doubt that millions of French citizens were in favour of the government of marshal Petain and took their orders from Vichy, a puppet government of the Germans).

The Germans reacted with extraordinary speed and sent in an unbroken stream of men under the command of General Juergen Von Armin, which included the powerful Hermann Goering armoured division and a battalion of tanks supplied with the fearsome Tiger I (a tank model which the Allies could only oppose with artillery or aircraft). Many analysts of the war believe that if Rommel had received half of these forces three months earlier, the outcome of El Alamein would have been entirely different.[22]

The battle for Tunisia is a clear example of how, so often, maintaining prestige is seen as more important than good sense.[23] Hitler's decision (late and wrong), far from being a solution, exacerbated the error. If he had wanted to retain his grip on North Africa, he should have done so in the sands of Egypt and the coast of Malta at the right time. The reinforcements which did not exist when and where they would have been the answer, at the key moment, appeared when it was too late, and so they ended up being wasted along with so many other resources (Map 5.2). Even so, the swift German reaction and bad weather thwarted hopes of a quick victory in North Africa before the end of 1942 and by mid-February 1943, the Germans were solidly dug in on the north and north-east coasts of Tunisia.

Rommel arrived in Tunisia to take command of the troops. In the meantime, the Allies gathered men and materiel for the final offensive while undertaking a range of operations designed to cut German communications. On February 16th Rommel attacked the inexperienced American soldiers, surprising them at the Kasserine pass. He soundly defeated them, but the battle was unimportant since he was unable to take advantage of his success. The Americans were soon to get over their first defeat on the African continent.

Map 5.2 End of the War in Northern Africa (1943).

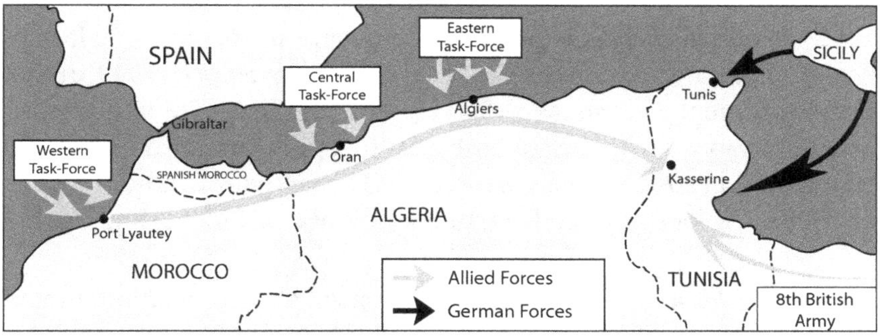

The Desert Fox, still quite ill, suggested to Hitler that he should withdraw his army to Italy to avoid a collapse before the Allies, but his suggestion was rejected and he was relieved of his command on March 8th.

Little by little the Allies won ground from the Germans and Italians whom they outnumbered and who could only be reinforced by sea with difficulty (the crossing between Sicily and Tunisia began to be known by Italian and German seamen as Death Route). In the wake of bitter fighting during April and May the Italians and Germans capitulated on May 13th, and 250,000 soldiers were taken prisoner, half of them German.

The southern flank of Europe, from Spain to Greece, was open to the Allies. Italy was completely exposed and was now the weakest link in the Axis chain.

4. All Roads Lead to Rome

Although it appeared the most logical step, the invasion of Italy caused disagreement between the British and the Americans. The Americans favoured a direct approach, landing in France, destroying the Germans and then advancing on Germany since they saw this as the shortest route to the defeat of their enemies.

The British, however, preferred an indirect approach, with less risk, which would continue to weaken the Germans and in the process might restrict any possible Soviet ambitions after the war. They proposed to attack the Balkans, the soft underbelly of the Nazi crocodile.

Both strategies had their pros and cons, and in the end a half-way house solution was adopted. France would be invaded in 1944, and in the meantime the Germans would be fought in Italy. This would also provide them with important air bases to bomb Germany, France and Romania (because the main source of German petrol came from the oil wells of Ploesti, in the Romanian province of Judetul Prahova).

It is very possible that had the invasion of France been attempted in 1943 it would have failed or cost huge casualties. On the other hand a landing in the Balkans with their awful communications and geographical barriers might have extended the war. In short, the decision that was taken may have been the correct one.

By mid-1943 the situation for Germany was becoming too complicated. It was already all but impossible for Germany to win the war, and the best that could be expected was a draw. Under these circumstances what looked like the best option to Guderian, Von Manstein and even Churchill, would be to set up a strong central reserve of 20 or 30 divisions which could be used at any critical point at any moment.

In this way Germany could take advantage of its central position from a geo-strategic point of view, and the German General Staff would be able to swiftly move its troops to concentrate them at the critical moment and destroy the Allies one at a time, before they could move on their own front. This had been the strategy adopted by Frederick II of Prussia when he defeated a coalition of powers (consisting of France, Austria, Sweden and Russia) as formidable as that which faced Germany in 1943.

However, as Churchill put it, "Hitler had in fact made a spider's web and forgotten the spider, he tried to hold everything he had won."[24] Sometimes it may turn out very convenient to withdraw, lose ground, market share, product lines, etc., in order to be still strong at the decisive point, at the key moment. As Von Manstein anticipated, "anyone who is not prepared to yield ground when necessary to save men, will also never find himself in a situation in which they can be strong enough at the decisive point."[25] Germany was behind an over-extended front, but his CEO couldn't see it, and was unwilling to sacrifice future success for current risk.

In 2004, the French company Thomson, famous for producing mass consumption electronics (mainly television sets), who sold the majority of their products in France, was haemorrhaging money and had a labour force of 65,000 workers world wide.

That was the year that Frank Dangeard took over the top management position and one of the first decisions he took was to sell off the television-manufacturing business to a Chinese firm and other consumer-electronics lines to Indian ones. Thomson concentrated on just one of the business lines: processing and transmission of images.

Four years later, by 2008, the company was selling only 4% of its services in France, and, although it had roughly the same turnover of 6 billion Euros, it was earning money steadily and had 21,000 workers on the payroll.[26]

In the same way, businesses like Germany in 1943 need to reinvent themselves from time to time, change their strategy, shifting their view to the bottom line, and concentrating on what is really important, even though it may appear painful in the short term, because the consequences of doing nothing are really leading to disaster.

After the conquest of Tunisia, the Allies had decided to invade Sicily, which was the gateway to Italy. On July 10th the Americans and British landed on the island, and after encountering stiff resistance (almost always and only from the Germans), they took Messina on August 17th, the last important city on the island. The Germans withdrew in good order with almost all their men, despite the Allied air and naval superiority.

During the invasion of Sicily, two important events had taken place. The first was that the momentum generated by the invasion itself acted to stop the German offensive at Kursk dead in its tracks (see Chapter 8), a fact that forced the Germans to realise that a second front had opened with full force.

The second was that on July 24th Mussolini was dismissed by means of a coup d'état from within. The actual governing body of the Fascist party fired its founder and president. The following day the King of Italy, the nominal Head of State, dismissed him from all his positions in the government and the Armed Forces.

The new authorities, headed by marshal Badoglio, announced that they would continue to fight alongside Germany while secretly negotiating with the Allies to change sides (coincidentally something very similar to what had happened in the First World War when, having established an alliance with Germany and Austria, they decided to enter the war on the side of the Allies and the Russians). For 45 days the Italians did almost nothing at all to halt the Allies who were meeting resistance only from the Germans who happened to be in Italian territory.

On September 3rd the British landed in the Italian peninsula, in Calabria. On the very same day, in absolute secrecy, an Italian delegation signed the surrender of Italy. Five days later an American army landed to the south of Naples, in Salerno, on the very day that the BBC announced that Italy had abandoned the war.

The Germans again reacted with their usual severity: they disarmed the Italian units (in Italy as well as France, Greece and Yugoslavia), annihilating them if they offered resistance, then freed Mussolini from gaol and threw themselves at the Salerno beachhead. They were within an ace of throwing the Americans into the sea, and it was only the decisive action of the naval guns and air support which prevented disaster.

With the danger stabilised, the Germans gradually withdrew towards the north, establishing a strong position on what was known as the Gustav line (a series of fortifications built by the Germans in Italy from the mouth of the river Garellano in the Tyrrhenian Sea to the mouth of the river Sangro in the Adriatic), where the slow Allied advance drew to a halt in December 1943.

The most strategic location on the Gustav line was on the slopes of Montecassino (near Rome), on the peak of which stood an abbey. From this highest point any Allied movement could be picked out so that artillery could be concentrated on it.

The Allies planned to make a frontal attack on the Gustav line, and, at the same time disembark their amphibious contingent behind the German lines. The landing point chosen was near the town as the Anzio and the date January 22nd 1944. At first things went well: there were no German troops between Anzio and Rome and the road to the eternal city was open. It looked as thought the Germans were about to be taken from behind on the Gustav line.

Even so, the American general in command of the troop landing was cautious and ordered the advance to halt to consolidate their gains before they continued forward. His strategy was simply to await events, and events were swift to make their presence felt.

The Germans drew strength from weakness and sending reinforcement from a number of fronts, on February 3 they moved to counter-attack. They launched furious charges against the Allies who on a number of occasions were on the point of wavering, and who, yet again, only stood firm thanks to the air and naval shelling.

By the beginning of March the danger for the Allies had passed, but they have achieved none of their objectives (they had neither liberated Rome nor broken the Gustav line). As Churchill was to describe later on, "I had hoped we were hurling a wildcat into the shore, but all we got was a stranded whale."[27]

A product launch or the start-up of a business with a novel service bears similarities to an amphibious landing. With no speed or manouvre they are probably doomed to failure. A good manager must have a clear strategic perception of what the next steps are, and at the same time, must be able to act with independence and initiative. If he is not ready for this, we can easily find that what has been so carefully planned, to which resources have been so judiciously allocated, and which has initially worked reasonably well, ends up as a very modest action, when not a failure.

If our rival is a powerful competitor, with experienced employees, tested resources and teams led by experts, we may find ourselves being pushed into the sea when everything had given the appearance that fate was about to smile on us. We always run the risk of allowing ourselves to be carried away by the temptation to do nothing, to relax and stay on the comfort zone side. All very well, it may not be a bad idea after all, but before we decide, we should listen to Churchill one more time: "surprise, intensity and speed are the essence of the amphibious landing. After 24 hours we may lose the advantage of having the sea power attack wherever it wishes. Where there were once ten men there are now ten thousand."[28]

In any case, and in the wake of the relative failure of the landing at the Germans' rear, the Allied generals re-adopted their method of the direct approach to the problem: frontal assaults on the Gustav line and Montecassino. On January 17th an attempt was made on the left flank, on January 20th on the centre and on the 24th on the north. Progress was small and casualties high. History repeated itself in February and March: frontal attacks, fresh slaughter and trivial results.

Faced with failure after failure a decision was taken in April to halt the butchery, reorganise the men and draw breath. The Allied generals realised that they could focus on the the same objective, but they must "not renew an attack along the same line after it has once failed."[29]

May 11th witnessed the fourth battle for Montecassino. After a well-coordinated series of attacks where the direction of the assault was different, a conclusion reached after a great deal of planning, a definite breakthrough was achieved. The monastery was taken on May 18th and almost without stopping, on May 23rd a decisive attack was launched on the Gustav line at the same time as an attack with the troops stationed in Anzio.

By May 25th 1944 the Germans were in full retreat, but even so the Allies failed to surround them and yet again they established themselves along the next line of defence, the Gothic line (a succession of defensive fortifications along the mountainous peaks of the Apennines which had been organised by marshal Albert Kesselring). On June 4th Rome was liberated by the American troops.

Two days later the Allies landed on the beaches of Normandy and the war in Italy clearly became of secondary importance for both sides (which does not mean that the intensity of the fighting was any the less, although the Allied advance halted for some months before the German lines, in this case the Gothic line). The situation remained stable, with slow and costly Allied gains and some partial breaches of the Gothic line.

It was not to be until April 1945 when the final offensive was launched which ended with the capitulation of the German army, now almost fighting in the Alps themselves, approximately a week before the end of the war in Europe. The final result of the Italian campaign is controversial.

From the German point of view, they had managed to organise things so that the Allies advanced slowly along the length of the peninsula without suffering any significant defeats. But the defence of Italy had meant that they had been obliged to devote men and materiel to this campaign, resources which otherwise could have had a significant effect in France or might have helped to stop the Soviets.

6

Other Fronts, Other Problems

1. The Importance of being Adolf

There were many countries involved in the defeat of German and Japan, but only three formed the Grand Alliance which finally won the war: Great Britain (and the Commonwealth), the Soviet Union and the United States of America. The three nations formed a coalition which the parallel war approach adopted by their enemies found invincible.

The three allies had formed a joint venture with the purpose of destroying Nazi Germany. In war, as in business, no such thing as a perfect leader exists, and there are different styles of leadership which may be successful at different times.

All managerial leadership requires a good administrative team which will make up for the shortcomings of the leaders. If possible, the members of this team should be chosen for their experience and qualities, and useless appointments based on political criteria should be avoided. Churchill, Roosevelt and Stalin, despite their many differences, were aware of this, and put it into practice.

But their great antagonist, Adolf Hitler, did not; his leadership style had at least three serious faults. In the first place, the *Führer* was unable to delegate, he was unable to appoint able, responsible chiefs to head each department. In the governmental cabinet there was no effective Prime Minister or energetic Head of the General Staff, jobs which had all ended up in his hands. He did not realise (or refused to see) that the time requirements for thought and strategy design are directly proportional to the height of the position.

Hitler deprived his forces of all initiative as the conflict proceeded. He interfered in the most trivial details of the battle, and regiments or air squadrons were shifted from one place to another at the instructions (or whims) of the supreme commander. The consequences were predictable. Hitler replaced overarching strategy by a mess of individual orders and decisions. At the same time, his military advisors were required to make a superhuman effort to mitigate the mistakes coming from his decisions and disagreements multiplied. The *Führer* dismissed anyone who disagreed with him or who refused to fight for every inch of ground.[1] And despite his exceptional responsibilities, Hitler never visited the front, striving to direct the war from a distance using a strategy which clashed catastrophically with the concept of mission command, a system which had provided excellent results for the Germans in the past.

Secondly, and as a direct consequence of this, he was unable to pace himself with his work, and burned out. Among the Allies there was no-one who dared take on even a small percentage of the *Führer*'s workload. Unaware of his limitations, he became increasingly inflexible and shut up inside himself. He subjected himself to an incessant mass of work to which he was unaccustomed. Since he launched the campaign in Russia, his former methods for solving problems, which consisted of getting rid of them all at one blow and then enjoying periods of leisure was replaced by endless days of work, each following the one before without a break. Where in the past he had been successful in getting others to do his work for him, now his problems ballooned because of his obsession with details. Although he saw himself as a disciplined worker, this was not in fact the case, and his disorganisation, exaggerated by too many responsibilities, hardly improved his ability to take decisions.

The excess of effort and isolation to which he subjected himself caused a strange state of insensibility and lack of feeling, tortured vacillation and never-ending irritability. He had to drive his exhausted brain to take the kind of decisions which in the past had been almost fun.[2]

The third fault was that when it came to choosing his team members, he used a form of negative selection to pick them. He had always tended to dismiss and replace those who had the audacity to contradict him as a matter of course, selecting more subservient individuals for the job in question, so that as the years passed he became more and more surrounded by people whose acceptance of his decisions was increasingly unquestioning, who executed them without demur.[3] He sought team members who were mere assistants, who would lose no time thinking about his orders and would merely hasten to obey them. This had a very negative effect on his operations.

His arbitrary decisions led to an absurd waste of the abundant and high quality expertise which was available to him. He dismissed, insulted, humiliated and imprisoned excellent workers, replacing them with faithful individuals whose only merit was that they followed his lead and saw things more optimistically and more positively than he did. Their level of skill was of little importance. The upshot was that he ended up surrounded by admirers who served only to cloud his judgement and in whom he would accept bad mistakes.

The outcome of all this was that the command structure, the management of the German Armed Forces, was chaotic and the primary reason for many defeats.

No General Staff as such actually existed. He appointed a group of officers to act as administrative assistants, whose business was to translate his decisions into orders, supplying him with information, but lacking the ability to design or recommend strategy. Strategic matters were analysed by the *Führer* together with a tiny gang of cronies from the Nazi party. The top commanders had no idea what to expect of their leader, and under such circumstances, they were deprived of any input in overall or long-term planning.

Nor was there any unity of command between Army, Navy and Air Force. The same could be said of all important areas of the war effort, production, logistics, human resources, intelligence, and so on, none of which was coordinated by a single committee or analysed by any type of war cabinet. No forum existed which could examine the war effort as a whole.[4] The three branches of the Armed Forces and the ministries were in competition with each other to seek power and the *Führer*'s favour, which in the final analysis was the sole common denominator of the war effort. And the *Führer*, far from striving for coordination actually encouraged these disagreements to gain his attention. His peculiar management style also ended up with his appointing two people to seemingly do the same job to compete for his favour, and usually the winner was the person who was most devotedly and single-mindedly consumed with the Führer's way.[5]

This being the case, what is surprising is the determination, ability and time that Germany was prepared to devote to the fight against the formidable coalition of enemies it faced. The only plausible explanation is that when the product is good and is in combination with a group of good professionals working for the company, not even a fanatic of Hitler's class is capable of destroying the business overnight.

Hitler's leadership is the evidence of what can happen in any business or organisation, never mind how soundly founded it is, if it ends up in the hands of a dreamer who cannot be held back, or an incompetent.

2. Weapons Secret and not so Secret

Throughout the entire conflict both Germany and Japan, perhaps because of their own weakness, were obsessed by the idea of possessing decisive weaponry on which they could stake everything in key battles and emerge victorious. As the years of the war passed and the likelihood of such a device appearing faded, so their faith in a miracle of this type grew. At the same time, on the other side, the situation was very different. The Allies had become convinced very soon that the war was going to turn into a marathon rather than a sprint, and had made their preparations accordingly.

They had therefore simplified the multitude of procedures with a view to being able to sustain the war as long as might be necessary. In the words of Hiroyoshi Ishibashi, founder of the Japanese weather-forecasting multinational Weathernews, when meteorologists claim to be 100% right, then their information will turn out to be 100%

irrelevant. Complicated plans are often just that, 100% irrelevant. What is simple is sometimes complicated, and what is complicated is often useless.

When we work out our strategic plans for the upcoming years, for example, we intend to start-up a business by ourselves, or we design a marketing or sales plan, we usually look for a "silver bullet": an iconic product or service, a final, devastating and original solution which will tip the scales. But such a silver bullet cannot emerge in an uncoordinated way and in a chaotic environment where everybody does as they please.

In Germany's case, because of the actual structure of the government, it was impossible to make a central, consistent and homogeneous plan. The various branches of the Armed Forces competed with each other, the ministries among themselves and each of them with the Armed Forces. Everybody was seeking their own silver bullet, everyone wanted to do "his own thing".

The outcome was that Germany produced weapons of very high quality, with levels of detail and finish which surprised friends as well as foes. But the effort of producing advanced weaponry came at a cost: a huge variety of projects competing for finance and attention and great difficulties in maintaining standardised production and sufficient output to tip the scales of the war.

For example, the Germans possessed more or less the same number of tanks and aircraft to attack the Soviet Union in 1941 as they had used to defeat the French and British in 1940. This factor made a decisive contribution to the survival of the Soviets in the first and critical six months of Operation Barbarossa.

At one time in the war, the German armed forces possessed no less that 425 models of aircraft, 151 different makes of lorry and 150 of motorcycles. This made mass production and the organisation of spare parts very difficult. Albert Speer, minister of armaments and war production since 1942, struggled hard to optimise this situation, and by applying simple solutions and common sense, he worked miracles. By 1944 there were 5 models of aircraft, 23 types of lorry and one single anti-tank weapon. This simplification process resulted in German weapons output reaching its maximum that year.[6] Unfortunately it was already too late for Germany.

In any case, technically the equipment available to the German army (jet aircraft, rockets, missiles, high performance submarines and tanks) was superior to that in the hands of its enemies. But this level of excellence was offset by the problem of the mass production of this equipment, which then meant that it was impossible to put sufficient quantities of them into the field to win the war. It was no use possessing top quality wood if it is only to be used for woodchips, particularly when faced with a well-protected enemy, ready for the counter-attack, who is wielding a tree-trunk.

To make things worse, until late into the war, Germany refused to restrict domestic consumption or to allow women to work in the factories in large numbers. Instead of this it made use of slave labour which it exploited ruthlessly, with low productivity and high mortality.

It seems as though the Germans were blinded by the quest for the silver bullet and failed to check whether they were sufficiently supplied with regular ones. But perhaps we ourselves are not immune to the allure of this idea. One of the first strategic decisions made by the CEO of the pharmaceutical giant GlaxoSmithKline (GSK), Andrew Witty, when he took over the position, was to attempt to lessen the obsession he identified in his company with blockbusters. The search for this silver bullet is like "finding a needle in a haystack right when you need it." The industry's reliance on risky blockbusters makes it vulnerable to "sudden torpedoes" in the form of lawsuits from generics firms, or regulatory crackdowns. Instead he proposed to look for many more potential drugs, both small and large, that can make up a more reliable pipeline. This will make GSK's drug-discovery efforts more akin to a nimble fleet of destroyers, rather than two or three vulnerable battleships.[7]

The Allies made things more simple. Unlike the German and Japanese secret services, whose inefficiency had resulted in their finding out very little more than thorough reconnaissance would have taught them, Allied intelligence succeeded in deciphering the German and

Japanese communication codes at a sufficiently early date for it to have a positive influence on events.

The majority of the messages transmitted between the various sections of each army were made by radio, which meant that it was essential to encrypt them to keep them secret because anyone with a receiver with the appropriate frequency could listen in to the transmissions.

The German armed forces were using the Enigma machine to encrypt radio and telegram messages. In theory, at least on paper, the 150 trillion possible configurations meant that its codes were to all intents and purposes unbreakable.[8]

In 1939 at Bletchley Park (near London) the British set up an office entrusted with the job of deciphering the Enigma machine. Within just a few months (the summer of 1940), with the help of some Polish experts who had fled the German invasion, mathematicians, cryptographers, linguists and bridge, chess and crossword devotees, they achieved what had seemed impossible: they could decipher German radio traffic with amazing regularity. And better still, the Germans never found out that their messages were being read in real time by the Allies until the war was over.

In practice, this meant that they were often aware of German movements before the actual German generals themselves knew. And this knowledge concerned not just the Armed Forces, but the Police and Diplomatic Service, too. Even today the real value of this information has hardly been assessed by historians, but there is no doubt that it saved thousands of Allied lives and considerably shortened the war. The war could never have been so greatly in the Allies favour in North Africa, the Atlantic or in Europe had they not been able to decipher the codes.

The Americans and the British were also able to decipher the codes and workings of the Japanese encryption machines and could decode both version Purple (for diplomatic purposes) and JN-25 [Japanese Navy 25, the version of the code used by the Japanese navy]. Hence Japanese communications were discovered and read as a matter of course from the very start of the war in the Pacific.

But the Allies had the advantage in more than just intelligence. Their industries were capable of producing more tanks, more aircraft, more guns and more ships than their opponents. This advantage alone was no guarantor of victory, just as being in possession of good financial clout does not necessarily mean that you will achieve your commercial goals, but it was a very positive step in that direction.

Both the Soviet Union and Great Britain achieved very praiseworthy successes (particularly in the case of the Russians, a large part of whose country had been invaded by the Germans). Both nations, each on its own account, managed to swiftly exceed Germany's armaments production. But it was to be the Americans who would tip the scale completely.

3. Welcome, Mr Marshall

On the morning of July 25th 1944 the elite armoured *Panzer Lehr* division of the German Army held a stretch of French countryside near the city of Saint Lô. For 49 days it had been struggling fiercely with the Allies following the Normandy landings, but its soldiers had no idea what was about to happen to them.

Suddenly the sky was full of waves of Thunderbolt fighter-bombers flying over them every two minutes, in groups of fifty, dropping high-explosive bombs and napalm incendiaries (highly inflammable petroleum jelly with a very long-lasting combustion quality).

They were followed by four hundred medium size bombers carrying 225 kilogram bombs. Then from the north came the sound every German soldier dreaded, they heavy drone of the big bombers – 1,500 Flying Fortress and Liberators. From their swollen bombs-bay 3,300 tons of bombs obliterated almost everything on the ground. Finally, the German line, or what was left of it, was pounded by three hundred Lightning fighter-bombers with fragmentation bombs and new incendiaries

And to round it off 10,000 American pieces of artillery pounded the few unfortunate members of the *Panzer Lehr* who were still this side of the grave. One of the few survivors recalled that it was like "being at sea during in a force 10 gale." The remains of the division stood in shock until the following day, when they were wiped out by American armour. [9]

The industrial power of the United States supplied a huge quantity of military equipment, arming all the armies confronting the Axis forces. But the Americans also provided millions of soldiers and sailors who were trained, equipped and prepared to confront a dangerous and resolute enemy.

How they achieved this is one of the most extraordinary stories of the Second World War which is often left behind in favour of bloody battles, secrets of the world of espionage, or the heroic deed of soldiers.

The Americans staked everything on making huge numbers of good quality materiel although not excellent. The brief was to produce in massive quantity, and to be practical. Let's compare the American M4 Sherman tank with the German Panzer VI Tiger I. An apocryphal version of the Sherman handbook said that "to tackle a Tiger you will need four Shermans, on the assumption that you will lose three."[10] But the fact was that 48,000 units were produced, compared to the Germans' production of 1,300 Tiger I tanks.

According to a calculation made by general Marshall, the United States transferred sufficient weaponry to its Allies to equip 588 armoured divisions, and 2,000 infantry divisions.[11] At the same time they equipped their own army of 8,000,000 men divided into 89 divisions: 66 infantry, 16 armoured, one of cavalry and one mountain division.[12] And these figures include neither the Marines fighting in the Pacific, nor the Air Force or the Navy.

And the data on the production of aircraft are even more spectacular. In 1944, the USA produced 96,318 aeroplanes of all kinds (a figure greater than the total capacity of the Axis, including German, Japanese and Italian production: twice the Russian output and nearly four times the British figure). The importance of air power was not just its ability to score victories in the field, but it also made it possible to aim powerful blows at the enemy's economy and at his land and sea communications.[13]

Naval output was no less remarkable. In comparison with the 392 large tonnage vessels built between Germany and Japan in 1943 (446 in 1944), the USA produced 2,654 vessels (2,247 in 1944).[14] This addition of war material tipped the balance simultaneously in both the Atlantic and the Pacific. For example, in barely 30 months, the combat fleet in action against the Japanese went from a strength of one aircraft-carrier, three cruisers and nine destroyers, to 18 aircraft-carriers, six battleships, 17 cruisers and 64 destroyers.[15]

But beyond the raw production data was the issue of training crews and officers, of setting up an effective logistical network in order to supply soldiers and sailors, of delivering this huge quantity of material. This meant that thousands of officers, sailors and soldiers had to be educated and trained.

Once again, the figures are remarkable. From 20,000 men in the Air Force in 1939, the figure rose to 2,400,000 in 1944 (of whom 12.5%, 300,000 individuals, were officers). Between 1941 and 1945 the Navy trained 286,000 officers. It was an unprecedented effort achieved with an amazing speed which surprised friends and foes alike.

How was it done? If you are in charge of an important company focusing on doing A (as the United States was before the attack on Pearl Harbour, an economy producing consumer goods) and a sudden change obliges you to change over to doing B (in this case, becoming the Arsenal of Democracy, in an economy completely orientated towards the war effort). What lessons can be learnt from the American mobilisation?

The first thing you will need are experts, managers with a wealth of technical and organisation skills. It was easy for the Americans to get access to the talent needed because the main American companies (especially those in the automobile sector such as Ford, General Motors or Chrysler) were very familiar with the organisation of huge mass production chains, and were staffed by management teams used to this sort of work.

The next thing you will need is for the management to be committed to the objectives, the ability to think big and conviction to make it happen (or in its contemporary political version 'Yes, we can', the motto which welded the American people together so that Barack Obama made it to the White House). This led to such phenomena as the "Liberty Ships" that were made in assembly-line style from prefabricated sections, so that the shipbuilding industry overcame the limitations of the shipyards. There were no mental barriers in the minds of the key personnel, just a commitment to make it, and inspirational optimism.

Europeans often see Americans as ingenuous, as having a simplistic, almost superficial, view of the world, one which leads them to tackle projects which are very complex with very basic ideas. Yet it was this simplicity of ideas, this unshakeable ingenuity, which allowed the United States to exceed all estimations regarding productive and military capacity.

Thirdly, you must allow initiative and innovation to be untrammelled. As we have seen, everything in the system allowed for initiative. Those in command (beginning with the President himself) delegated and strove to avoid interfering in matters of lesser importance. Once strategy and objectives have been defined, you must let the experts do their work.

They were inspired leaders, leaders who knew how to delegate, who left technical problems to those who really knew how to solve them, who concentrated on what they did best and kept mental obstacles out of their plans. As Henry Ford said, "whether you believe you can, or you believe you can't, you're right."[16, 17]

Summing up, the three important lessons to be learnt are relatively simple (although they need a genuine commitment on your part to put them into practice): surround yourself with experts, a decent handful of innovators, ask for commitment (and don't be carried away by prejudices) and promote mission command.

The Americans completely trusted their potential, they had a shared commitment, and they had the technical skills, able people and the commitment to success. Why wouldn't they be able to achieve their goal? And in fact, they did.

4. The Battle of the Atlantic

For the Germans the most effective indirect strategy to defeat the British and Americans was to break the lines of communication which crossed the Atlantic.

If they had succeeded, the British would have been starved into submission, the Russians could not have mounted their 1942 and 1943 offensives and all the industrial and human power of the American would have been useless, as it would have ended up at the bottom of the sea.

The Atlantic was the Gordian Knot of the Allied machine, the Achilles' heel of the Americans, of the British Nestor (the respected counsellor of the Greeks at the Trojan war) and the Russian Colossus. We have already mentioned the advantages of the indirect approach. For eminent military strategist Basil Henry Liddell Hart the indirect strategy is always the "most hopeful and economic strategy."[18] What the Germans needed to do was to try to cut down the enemy, where they were most vulnerable, so that they would lose their balance and come crashing to the ground. And this should be done in the most economic way possible.

While this may appear a fairly obvious strategic decision, it is very surprising that the Germans afforded such low importance (relatively) to this part of the war. The British, aware of what was at stake, were definitely in fear of a German deployment which would cut their communications with the Americans. Churchill stated that "the only thing that ever really frightened me during the war was the U-boat peril."[19]

There were two key aspects to the battle in the waters of the Atlantic. The first was the British decision to proclaim the Battle of the Atlantic as a necessary measure demanding all levels of combat importance on that front, despite the fact that (or rather precisely because) it was a day-to-day, self-sacrificing struggle, with no grand headlines, based on steadiness and everyday work.

This proclamation had the effect of allowing for the concentration of human and equipment resources in the struggle, soon to be reinforced by the entry of the Americans into the fray. Interdisciplinary groups were formed and the highest military and civil levels were involved in the achievement of a common objective.

In other words, the first thing we must understand is the basic problem which afflicts our organisation. It may be that the problem is not the kind that can be solved by a brilliant and lighting action of the kind that wins medals, so beloved by our executives. And it may be that it is not the favourite problem of our CEO, despite the fact that the future of our business is riding on it.

So, a good solution is to proclaim our own Battle of the Atlantic and to ask our teams to focus on it, despite their daily agenda, setting up regular de-briefings on the project, so that no one forgets about the relevance of the battle. Just like Winston Churchill, for battles such as this, you will need to set up a working team of your own.

Secondly, once the objective has been defined and the problem identified, it is important (once again) to maintain concentration and not to lose the vision. Yet again, we see how the Germans scattered their resources, and when they managed to concentrate them, they ended up losing the vision and abandoning it at the first opportunity. As Thomas Edison said, "Many of life's failures are people who did not realize how close they were to success when they gave up."[20]

On the other hand, the Allies maintained a single consistent strategic line throughout the conflict, despite bitter disagreements and attempts to change it.

When war broke out, the Germans were clearly in an inferior position as regards warships compared to the French/British. This inferiority persisted until the fall of France and the conquest of Norway, as they had a very small number of submarines and for the most part they were bottled up in the Baltic (where they were capable of very little). But after 1940, things began to change.

With the French fleet neutralised and access to the French ports (and the Norwegian), the submarines could reach almost any target in the Atlantic, particularly in the zones where there was no air protection for the Allies. Between June and November 1940 one merchant ship after another was sunk, totalling 1,600,000 tons of cargo (amounting to 266,000 tons per month), impressive figures if you bear in mind the fact that this was achieved by rather less than 60 submarines which were never all in action at the same time (some would on training duties, others under repair or inspection, so that the remainder had to spread out through the various theatres of the naval struggle).

Despite their successes, the Germans devoted few resources to the naval battle. In 1940, 48 submarines were delivered to the German Navy [Kriegsmarine] and although in 1941 the increase was significant (186 new vessels) the number was still too low. They were also under-used and the great possibilities opened up by working with the Air Force after the conquest of France were wasted. In the words of Admiral Doenitz, "the German Navy fought without aerial reconnaissance and without its own aircraft, as if the aeroplane had never been invented."[21]

Nor did this situation bode well for surface warfare, and as a consequence of this lack of foresight, German warships also failed to bother the British Navy. And this was in spite of the fact that at the beginning of the war, they had been able to strike hard. In naval guerrilla actions they had sunk a large number of British vessels, both mercantile and warships, and given their inferiority in surface craft, these were significant results.

These actions were a real headache for the Admiralty, the command of the Royal Navy, and caused them to lose concentration on the anti-submarine war, from where they diverted important resources.

In one skirmish, in May 1941, the battleship Bismarck was sunk (a vessel which had inflicted huge damage on British shipping, to the point that Churchill had given the order that the Bismarck must be sunk at all costs). Hitler was so incensed by this that he gave the order that no surface vessel should go into action without his express permission, and this was never given, except for very limited actions. The British must have been delighted by the Führer's latest order.

Aware of these weaknesses, the Royal Navy, developed a long term, consistent and sound strategy, supporting what had been proclaimed as the Battle of the Atlantic. The technical systems for detecting submerged submarines were improved (thanks to upgrades in the sonar equipment). Convoy protection tactics were also buttressed by the use of escort vessels such as corvettes, smaller and cheaper craft than destroyers and which did the job almost as well as them (of around 1,000 tons compared with the 3,000 tons of a destroyer, the 15,000 tons of a cruiser and the 70,000 of a battleship). The convoy system, was adopted both in the First and Second World Wars as the most effective way of protecting the merchant ships. It consisted of grouping the merchant vessels together and protecting them with warships during their sea passage so that they could hunt submarines while still performing protection duties, instead of fruitlessly searching for U-boats in the immensity of the Atlantic.[22]

As a response to this defensive technique and with the resources of the German Navy concentrated exclusively on the submarines, the Germans, headed by the Commander of the Submarine Fleet, the innovator Karl Doenitz, developed a new tactic: the "Wolf Pack".

Traditionally the submarines attacked the convoys by day and sub-merged, acting alone and following their commanders' instructions. The new technique was for the submarines to attack the convoys in groups, the wolf packs, by night and on the surface. In this way they could not be located by sonar or radar, which together with the darkness of the night meant that they were difficult of find. The com-bination of several attack points (because they were a group) sowed confusion among the escorts.

By 1941 the situation was a draw. The Allies held their ground thanks to the establishment of air bases equipped with aircraft which patrolled large areas of the Atlantic, to the use of the Ultra machine which deciphered the codes transmitted by the Germans with their Enigma (which allowed them to dodge the concentrations of the wolf packs) and to the provision by the United States of 50 destroyers at a time when the Admiralty's resources were stretched to the limit.

The entrance of the USA into the war meant a fresh threat for the submarines but also a great opportunity since the wolf packs' paws could now extend to all coasts and seas, setting aside the enormous care they had hitherto taken to avoid American shipping (it had not been forgotten that it was the sinking of The Lusitania which had brought the United States into the First World War in 1917 and Hitler had been determined not to provide the same motivation yet again).

The Germans grasped this new opportunity with their usual efficiency. Nursemaid submarines came into service (known as Milk Cows) to supply the wolf packs, carrying enough provisions and torpedoes to keep twelve submarines in action for two months without their having to touch land.

At the beginning of 1942, Doenitz had nearly 250 submarines operational. Optimism was at such a high level that one of the German commanders predicted a speedy denouement: "We shall give the Americans the last rites." Indeed, for some months the results were spectacular, and it appeared as though the German submarines were invincible. Between January 1942 and mid-April 250 American vessels were sunk for the loss of just one submarine. The Allies were very worried, because if they could keep it up at this rate, the Germans would soon have the Western Allies out of the game, leaving the Russians seriously weakened.

But yet again Germany lost her momentum. Just when the battle was at its height, with the Americans more or less defenceless, Hitler insisted on sending submarines to prevent a hypothetical invasion of firstly the Azores, and then Norway. Neither of these invasions would ever have taken place.

Winston Churchill recounts in his memoirs: "The U-boat attack was our worst evil. It would have been wise for the Germans to stake all upon it. I remember hearing my father say 'in politics when you have got hold a good thing, stick to it'. This is also a strategic principle of importance."[23]

The brief respite this allowed gave the Americans time to catch their breath (mainly to adopt the same measures as the British had been deploying for over a year). Little by little losses fell. And thanks to the prefabricated ships, sinkings were to some extent offset by new launchings, which was something that Germans had not foreseen.

132

By the summer of 1942 the tables were beginning to turn. Attacks on the Allies became increasingly dangerous and less profitable. The Americans learned fast and had the capacity necessary to be able to invest huge resources in the fight, while all the experience accumulated by the British was beginning to pay off.

New inventions were soon in action, together with upgraded versions of those already in existence, and the Allies kept relentlessly on the right path. More sophisticated radar so that submarines on the surface could be detected by aircraft as well; the radio direction finder (an electronic system capable of determining the direction of a radio signal) whereby it was possible to track down any broadcast up to 25 miles away, so that when U-boats communicated to form a wolf pack, the convoys could simply avoid the submarines; long-haul aircraft taking off from new air bases; escort aircraft-carriers; and multiple depth charges.

But even so, the second half of 1942 was still very tough for the Allies. Between June and November over 800,000 tons was sunk on average per month (the other months the figure was a no less disturbing 600,000 tons of losses per month). The change was that now the Germans were paying very dearly in sunk submarines (nearly 90), which also meant above all a loss of experienced crews.[24]

1943 began with the German appointment of Doenitz as Commander-in-Chief of the *Kriegsmarine*, and with over 200 submarines operational and more under training. Hitler gave orders that submarine building efforts should be intensified and their quality improved.

Unfortunately for the Germans, the Allies were now too strong, and the systematic, quiet and rational strategy on which so much work and effort had been expended was beginning to bear fruit.

That year the tables began to turn, and despite the 3,220,137 tons of shipping which had been sunk (579 vessels), the Germans had lost 237 submarines. And what was more, the Allies had launched over thirteen million tons (in other words losses were around 25%, still a high percentage, but much lower than previous figures). In 1944 and 1945 German submariners hardly managed to sink 1,500,000 tons.[25]

The Allies had been able to identify their main problem and find a response to it, which was neither immediate nor easy. In the meantime, the Germans had lost their chance through being unable to assess the importance of the struggle at the right time. They were unable to maintain the vision and their concentration at a time when, had they been able to do so, it might have been the factor which tipped the balance in their favour.

Even so, the figures for Germany show how hard the fight had been and how it could have gone either way. Doenitz sent 863 submarines into battle (of these he lost 630) which sank 148 warships and 2,279 merchant ships. The strategic importance is not revealed by the actual figures, however, since it tied up more than 3,000 vessels and over 5,000 aircraft which, logically, could have been deployed in other fronts.[26]

5. Strategic Bombing

When the time had come to attempt to put an end to the war, the British and the Americans felt that an indirect approach would be a good way to achieve a final victory. For this purpose they selected a strategic bombing strategy, an idea that, at least on paper, was very good.

The plan was to bomb the enemy's factories, their oil refineries, their oil wells, their rail junctions and their largest cities, the aim being to disrupt the enemy's economy so that the armies would grind to a halt for want of spare parts, munitions and fuel. The civilian population would also suffer a crisis of morale so that their leaders would have no option but to sue for peace.

The basis of the idea was to avoid costly land battles, since the memory of the First World War and the slaughter on the Western Front was still very much alive. In the previous conflict, the fighters at the front lines were killed off age group by age group, by the ability of both sides to produce a never ending supply of machine guns, ordnance, and artillery munitions. The new solution being suggested was therefore completely sensible: if we stop the assembly lines and the factories, the enemy will have to surrender and there will be no need to fight bloody battles.[27]

The idea was far from new, and had actually been used by the Germans at the beginning of the war, when, in 1939, they had bombed Warsaw, Rotterdam, and later on the United Kingdom during the Battle of Britain, with a view to destroying the enemy's morale. At the end of 1940 the only possibility for Great Britain to win the war was, in Churchill's words, "an absolutely devastating, exterminating attack by heavy bombers from this country upon the Nazis."[28]

But this was just wishful thinking. The British lacked sufficient aircraft, and those they had were unable to carry sufficient bombs; and anyway, they would be unable to locate their objectives or to hit them accurately, since they would have to fly by night to minimise losses.

This meant that the British attacks in 1940 and 1941 were no more than pinpricks as far as German cities and industry were concerned. And the Royal Air Force soon started to take serious losses when the Germans adopted various kinds of countermeasures, mainly deploying night fighters with the support of radar and anti-aircraft systems. 492 aircraft were shot down in 1940 and 1,034 in 1941.[29] It was a high cost to achieve almost nothing.

In 1942, in spite of everything, the balance tipped in favour of the supporters of strategic bombing. This was basically for two reasons. The first was the appointment of Arthur "Bomber" Harris (also known as Arthur "Butcher" Harris by his RAF comrades) as head of Bomber Command. His appointment occurred at the same time that new and better aircraft were made available to him. Harris was an expert, a rather reserved individual, somewhat austere, but hardworking and persevering. Despite the fact that many analysts feel he was not particularly brilliant, he was certainly capable of defending his department. He also methodically put together the resources he felt were necessary, seeking out (and finding) the technical means required for the necessary operational efficiency.

Since the aircraft were unable to hit the selected targets with precision, he opted for "carpet bombing" (also known as area bombing) which consisted of attacking whole cities instead of specific targets. For this purpose new bombs were produced, particularly incendiaries, designed to cause mass destruction instead of precision.

New bombers also came into service, heavier aircraft which carried larger, heavier bombs to more distant destinations. As well as that, new tactics also came into play, with lighter aircraft, Pathfinders, which led the attacking force and illuminated the target for the heavy bombers that followed, thus simplifying the pilots' work.

In the second place, the Americans arrived. This meant that an unprecedented quantity of resources were available for Bomber Command, both human and materiel. And again the Americans were bursting with confidence; "let's show these English how you win a war," they said. However, during 1942 they limited their work to gaining experience by attacking targets in France with the combined support of fighters before the actual offensive in 1943.

In spite of everything, 1942 brought the Allies no positive results and losses among the British night bombers continued to be very high. However, the change in strategy certainly meant bad news for the German civilians when they found themselves the target of the bombs. If German industrial capacity could not be destroyed, the Allies reckoned, at least the morale and the homes of the citizens could. As a result, thousands of German civilians were killed and their homes destroyed. Yet these attacks neither undermined German morale nor did they force the Nazi leaders to call London begging for peace.

In 1943, new energies were put to the fight. The Allies now had an impressive fleet of aircraft and were able to attack a target with up to 2,000 aircraft on single mission.

In addition to this the American Eighth Air Force was now in a position to take action against Germany. Equipped with B17 aircraft, known as Flying Fortress, they were theoretically capable of defending themselves against the fighters and resisting the impact of anti-aircraft ordnance, so night missions were now no longer necessary. Bombing in broad daylight meant avoiding the need for carpet bombing so there was no wastage of hundreds of bombs to hit a target, which allowed more selective attacks on rail communications junctions and sources of supply of raw materials and fuel.

The objective was firstly to paralyse German industry and the flow of supplies to the front, then the destruction of German cities and the civilian population's will to fight on; and by way of a coda, the end of the war. Americans would bomb by day and the British by night. Germany would have no rest.

However, the reality was somehow different, the Americans were suffering terrible losses and the bombing was not having the desired effect. Although on average they lost 5% of their aircraft on each mission, there were some occasions when they lost as much as 60%. This fact meant that, statistically and in the best case scenario, a pilot could hardly survive 20 missions. But even worse, German industry far from being paralysed, was in fact increasing production.

In any case, the Allies earned an unexpected bonus from their insistence. The Germans had to withdraw their precious *Luftwaffe* from other theatres of war to defend their skies and their cities. By 1943, 70% of German fighters were involved in the defence of the *Reich*, together with a good proportion of anti-aircraft guns and human resources. This was a huge relief for the Soviets at a time of great danger for them.

The destruction of the cities and the loss of German civilian lives continued, but so did the German war effort, and it seemed as though the bombing had had no effect on industry, morale or transportation in Germany.

By the beginning of 1944 it began to look as though the Allies had failed and would have to abandon the campaign and halt the strategic bombing due to the high number of losses, particularly among the Americans. But a new advance tipped the scale. The Allies had developed a new fighter, the P-51 Mustang, able to escort the bombers on their missions over German territory.

With this new protection, losses of American bombers fell dramatically. The bombing continued to have no significant effect on German productivity or morale, but by the spring of that year the *Luftwaffe* had been beaten.

By April 1944, the *Luftwaffe* was noting an alarming loss of pilots to replace and there were barely enough aircraft to cover the continuous losses caused by the defence of the German cities. The imbalance of fighters on the Western Front was one to seven, while on the Eastern Front it was one to nine Soviet aircraft.[30] The German air force was in a state of collapse, running out of aircraft and pilots.

With the *Luftwaffe* almost annihilated, after a short breather to support the Allied landings in France, the Bomber Command decided to recommence its efforts over Germany. Cities and factories, the transportation system, oil refineries, all were flattened almost unopposed, causing serious human and equipment losses. But Germany fought on…

What had initially been planned as a campaign to destroy the morale and the industry of the *III Reich*, had positive consequences for the Allies as it forced the enemy to devote so much in the way of resources to the defence of his own territory that it weakened him on the really decisive fronts (the Russian Front, and after June 1944, the Western Front).

This was exactly how Speer himself, minister for German industry, saw it when he stated that "the bombing-campaign did not excessively harm either production or morale, but they wasted aircraft and anti-aircraft resources (and anti-tank equipment in the case of the guns) which could have been used on other fronts, particularly the Russian Front."[31]

But Germany pulled out all the stops to increase the production of tanks, aircraft and guns right up to the end of 1944. The analysis of the Americans after the war concluded that the policy of razing industrial and inhabited zones had proved to be a failure: "it did not substantially affect the course of German war production. German war production as a whole continued to increase and morale of the civilian population was not destroyed".[32]

Although it might be even more surprising to observe that, having maintained their concentrated effort, perhaps the Allies had managed to paralyse the German effort in a meaningful way. Albert Speer himself admitted that the massive Allied bombing did on occasions put the German war effort on the ropes, but the lack of continuity and the insistence on the same objectives resulted in no definitive results being achieved.

Speer calculated that if they had concentrated their efforts in a sustained manner over the period upon five or six actual and relatively small targets (factories producing ball bearings or bearings, for example, parts essential for the manufacture of motors) the effect of the bombing could have been really damaging.[33] The problem was that the Allies changed their objective when they were on the point of success.

Summing up, it can be said that despite the so-called strategic bombing of Germany achieving none of its initial objectives it had a genuinely beneficial effect which really did impact the progress of the war, in that it destroyed the *Luftwaffe*, forcing Germany to devote a vast quantity of resources to the anti-aircraft battle (which was ultimately to fatally weaken her position on other open fronts). The negative side, of course, was the death of hundreds of thousands of German civilians.

Sometimes maintaining the vision is more important than the strategy being right. Companies often provide executives with a large amount of human and equipment resources in quest of a strategic objective, but then abandon it at the first setback. Not yielding to these initial difficulties and not trying to achieve other objectives at the same time will prevent us from giving up the game when it may be that not much remains to be done to achieve success… even though the objective may not be achieved.

Maintain your vision, you may not succeed in causing your particular Germany to surrender, but there is no doubt that you will achieve some positive effect like the destruction of the *Luftwaffe*, which may lead to the collapse of your enemy.

7

Overlord: the Normandy landings

1. Preparations

It seemed to the Western Allies that the fastest and most direct way to win the war was to confront the bulk of the German Armed Forces in France, and once they had been defeated, to advance swiftly on Germany at the same time as the Soviets were doing so from the east. This meant doing the opposite of what Philip II of Spain, Napoleon and even Hitler himself had unsuccessfully attempted.

The direct approach strategy involved serious risks. Were it to fail, it could mean the total or partial victory of the Germans. At least it would buy them some precious time, which would prolong the war in a terribly bloody fashion. The Americans preferred this solution over the prudence of the British. They had at last reached a consensus solution which, hindsight would reveal, was the right one. The entire operation was designed according to the maxim which has so often inspired people to fight for their dreams, "there are no impossible tasks, there are no unreachable goals."

Leaving dreams aside, once the decision had been taken, they had to work out how to do it. We are all capable of being very creative and producing wonderful ideas, but "98% of innovation is implementation."[1]

It was obviously very difficult to place on the other side of the English Channel a force with sufficient battle capacity to first defeat the Germans and then clear a way to the German border. Efforts would be pointless if the battalions were not kept well supplied at all times, which would demand even more force, since everybody was aware of the fact that the Germans would dynamite all the ports, airports, bridges and railway lines as the withdrew.

Paradoxically, the problem of location of the landing was one of the simplest of all. In theory the invasion could take place at any point between the Spanish frontier and Norway, but a rigorous analysis of the possibilities cut this down to two zones: Normandy and Calais.

The head of the attack required an area with wide beaches where the formidable amphibious forces which were to be mobilised could be landed. It was also necessary to be able to guarantee effective cover from the fighters and tactical aircraft based in England. The Brittany peninsula was rejected because the landed troops could be cut off from the rest of France with relative ease. So the best points for the attack were, as the majority of the Germans suspected, somewhere between Normandy and Calais.

The Allied experts had started the long and difficult work of preparation, a task which, especially as regards logistics, took years. Since 1942 a working group had been analysing the possibilities and requirements for the invasion.

Finally Normandy was chosen because, despite having worse air cover and requiring a longer sailing time, it had weaker defences than Calais, the beaches were satisfactory, and once the attack had been launched it would be relatively easy to isolate and capture the port of Cherbourg. A landing in this zone would also give the Allies relatively good communications with the interior of France and prevent them from being enclosed after D-Day (the code name for the landing date).

The Allies put themselves in the shoes of the German generals, anticipating their reasoning and deducing that the Germans would locate fewer defensive resources in the zone. This was because between Cherbourg and Le Havre there were 50 miles with wide, sandy beaches, so an attempt to land there would certainly have limited possibilities of success. It was true that they could land a force of some 20,000 men there without difficulty, but without a port available to them there was no way they could be supplied or reinforced with the necessary speed, and they would be annihilated before they built up sufficient capacity to take the port of Cherbourg or Le Havre.

The Allies, however, felt that they could take the Germans by surprise. It was an ideal solution except for that one detail, they needed a port so that they could supply the troops and avoid being isolated and at the mercy of the enemy. But how could they get a port where there was none?

The experts talked for weeks, yes, Normandy looked like a good location, but without the least guarantee of supporting port after the landing the option was an illusion. When they were on the point of rejecting the option, someone wondered out loud whether it would be possible to build a port out of parts and tow it to its destination. The comment drew derisory snorts, but a mere two years later that crazy idea was a reality.[2]

The solution consisted of two, large scale, artificial ports to be towed into position and which would go into action within a few days of the landing. They would be known as Mulberries. With this problem sidestepped, Normandy was now the perfect place (Map 7.1).

However, the Allies' innovation did not stop there. They built amphibious tanks, vehicles capable of opening a path through minefields and attacking fortifications with flamethrowers, an oil pipeline was designed to connect England with the front itself in France. The Germans were able to oppose this kind of imagination and innovation with only the traditional forms of defence. The result was that while the Allies understood the "no important problem can be solved with the same level of thinking in which it arose,"[3] the Germans were locked into trying to.

The man placed at the head of this huge deployment was general Dwight "Ike" Eisenhower, an officer who had already led the Allies on the first joint campaigns in Tunisia and Italy. Ike's military career had been relatively humdrum and little in it hinted that he was destined to pass into the pages of military history as one of the foremost military chiefs of all times.

Map 7.1 Normandy or Calais? (1944)

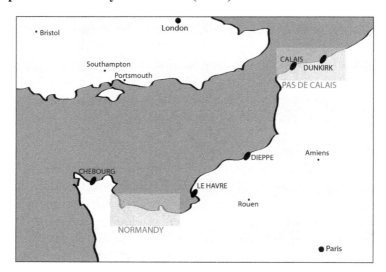

Although he was not a particularly brilliant strategist, his qualities included an outstanding ability as an organiser, and above all, as a coordinator who knew how to win the cooperation of all his men. He kept the coalition of forces united and of one mind, and thanks to his conciliatory management style, he understood that the key was to minimise disagreements between the Allies and to keep then focused on the achievement of the military objectives.

He worked to coordinate and simplify procedures, getting rid of needless bureaucracy so that efforts could be concentrated on what really mattered. Keen on the concept of "a coordinated programme with a single head,"[4] he also banked on the fact that "true delegation implies the courage and readiness to back a subordinate to the full"[5] and placed his trust in mission command in order to avoid "imposing rigidity of action upon the commander who receives orders for execution."[6]

Battles and business decisions are often taken in an environment of "the fog of war", with no other way than to take a decision based on calculations and possibilities, not objective, real facts. The result of this fog will be the first setbacks.

If you find yourself in this situation, Ike's recommendation is to radiate calm and optimism which clarifies disputes, doubts and uncertainties because "In such circumstances it is always necessary for the commander to avoid an attitude of defeatism; discouragement on the part of the high commander inevitably spreads rapidly throughout the command and always with unfortunate results."[7]

Colin Powell Chairman of the Joint Chiefs of Staff in the first Gulf War (later to become Secretary of State), agrees, stating that even though optimism is an important multiplying force, cynics and pessimists are always in a majority. He recalls the kind of people who defend themselves with a lack of data, yet who would never have all the data, and if ever they did, it would in all probability be too late. Decisions have to be taken when you think you have between 40% and 70% of the possibilities worked out: before then, it would be too risky, and afterwards, simply too late.[8]

Fine, but whereabouts between that 40% and 70%? Trust your instinct. Napoleon said "In war there is but one favourable moment; the great art is to seize it!" The experts will always have more data than judgement, so never let yourself be too intimidated by them. The war in Europe was won because "through every trial and every temptation… (the decision makers) never wavered from their purpose"[9]; they maintained their vision right up to the end, neither daunted by imminent catastrophes, nor excited by brilliant victories.

But let's get back to England in mid-1944, where the Allies were ready to invade mainland Europe. There were 20 American divisions, 17 from Great Britain and the Commonwealth, one French and one Polish; 5,049 fighter planes, 3,467 heavy bombers, 2,343 aircraft of other kinds, 2,316 air transports and 2,591 gliders. In addition there was a fleet of over 6,000 ships and landing craft.[10] All in all, almost three million men in perfect order awaiting the order to go into battle.

Although some were battle-hardened veterans, the majority were, as Churchill says in his Memoirs, "officers and men who were going into battle for the first time yet who behaved like military experts."[11] Not for nothing had they been methodically trained, their lengthy apprenticeship covering not only combat itself, but also communications, logistics, coordination and organisation.

They were also in possession of detailed information about the zone, thanks to a huge effort on the part of military intelligence to compile information about the area. In addition to millions of aerial photographs there was the information provided by the submarine patrols sent out to the landing zones, regular documentation supplied by French spies, and more. But other documentation was also examined in case it could supply information which had been missed, from tourist guides to pictures take from British tourists before the war (about 10,000 were examined).

Two days after the invasion, the officers of the General Staff of the *Hitlerjugend Panzer* division were able to examine the documentation found in a Canadian tank destroyed that morning. "We were flabbergasted to see such a degree of exactness. The fortified points were all perfectly pinpointed, with a list of the weapons defending them, including light machine guns and mortars."[12]

In addition, we should not forget that the Allies were decoding German wireless communications in real time (Enigma decoding).

To combat that impressive deployment, the German Army had, on paper, 58 divisions. The reality was that many of them existed in the weakest possible condition (in many cases they were manned by reservists of up to 40 years of age, the sick, convalescents recovering from wounds received on the Eastern Front, the handicapped and foreigners such as Russians, Armenians, Georgians and the like, with uncertain devotion to the cause).

More serious yet was the command situation. Get a pen and paper, you're going to need it… General Von Rundstedt, the experienced expert from the campaigns in France and the Soviet Union, was now Commander-in-Chief of the *Werhmacht* in France. But Rommel was in charge of the groups of armies, which covered the coast between Brittany and the Netherlands, and although he was nominally under the command of Von Rundstedt, he was reporting directly to Hitler. In his turn, Goering was controlling the airborne and anti-aircraft units from Berlin, while Himmler was the overall commander of the *Waffen SS* (the combat division of the SS, the Nazi party's Praetorian Guard, which tacitly was supposed to act under the control of the

Werhmacht). To cap it all, the *Panzer* divisions, which constituted the strategic reserve, were under Hitler's direct command and were supposed to act only under his express decisions. Compared with an Allied system of a single programme and a single head, the Germans had a mass of commanders… and programmes.

Rommel was in favour of a forward defence: near the coast, given that the first 24 hours would be crucial. During those initial hours, the enemy would have had no time to concentrate and could not take advantage of its air power, which otherwise would prevent the Germans form undertaking any daylight moves. He knew the Americans and the British. He had fought with them in the Mediterranean and was familiar with the devastating effects of their air superiority. With this in mind, he made a huge effort to garrison the coast under his control, involved his men in continuous training exercises and exhausting fortification work and even came up with all kinds of devices to slow down the invasion (like very cheap, easily manufactured anti-tank obstacles, known as "Rommel's asparagus", and mines encased in porcelain to avoid scarcity of metals).

The chief risk of this strategy was that, at the time of the invasion, the German forces were too spread out to resist a mortal blow from the invader. The fact that the Germans were also uncertain about the exact location of the invasion meant that his arguments were even more open to question. Naturally, the Allies would sustain this uncertainty as long as possible, even intensifying the bombing of Calais (dropping two bombs for every one they dropped in Normandy) and concentrating a fake army corps in the vicinity of Dover to reinforce the theory of an invasion on the beaches of Calais.

Even so, Rommel insisted that despite the scattered deployment of the German troops, they would still retain their superiority if at the decisive moment they attacked within a few hours of the landing.

On the other hand, Von Rundstedt had a more conventional view, more that of the expert. According to his strategy, victory was to be achieved by deploying a few divisions on the coast to absorb the initial attack, and as soon as the direction of the attack was known, he would launch a powerful counter-attack at the beachhead with devastating results. This strategy involved the risk that the mobile units of the reserve might not arrive in time to achieve complete superiority over the enemy in terms of air power.

In the end a compromise – not a consensus decision – was reached, imposed by Hitler himself, who once again had taken on complete strategic and tactical responsibility for the situation. The mobile reserve was placed behind the beaches (as Von Rundstedt wished) and the rest of the forces scattered along the coast (as Rommel preferred). Hitler's decision made a fragile defence yet feebler: there were too few mobile divisions in the reserve to have a punch effect, and too few of them near the coast to fight the invaders on the beaches.[13]

And to add insult to injury, Hitler insisted on building powerful fortifications and positions garrisoning forces along the length of the north coast of Europe (twelve divisions in Norway and another six in Denmark) spreading out the men and resources too thinly, in a way that Germany could barely afford.

As the spring progressed, the Germans knew that the time for landing was approaching (it had to be at the end of the spring or the beginning of the summer). They also knew that in all probability it had to be somewhere between Normandy and Calais (this was proved by the intensity of the bombing and the concentration of troops and materiel in England). All they needed to know was exactly where and when. That information was already known in London. The landing was to be on the beaches of Normandy on June 5th 1944.

2. D-day and H-hour

By Saturday June 3rd everything was ready for the invasion, which was to be launched on the 5th. However, disturbing information about the weather was arriving at Eisenhower's office: in the wake of the three previous weeks of good weather, the situation looked frankly poor for June 5th and 6th. A period of one day was set as a margin for taking the decision. At 4.00 am on Sunday June 4th it looked as though the weather was never going to improve, and Ike decided to postpone the whole operation "for at least 24 hours".[14]

Barely five hours later (at 9.15 am) he reassembled his commanders to take a decision as to whether the landing could be made on the 6th or not. At that moment it was raining hard and there was quite a lot of wind. Eisenhower asked for advice and listened carefully to the representatives of Armed Forces. While the Air Force chiefs erred on the side of prudence, the Army chiefs wanted to try and launch the attack. The naval reports were more decisive: "We have 30 minutes to decide, otherwise we have to delay the entire operation, perhaps by a month if we want the best moon and tide conditions". (Optimum conditions for the landing and offering no advantage to the German defence had been established as: full moon, with a short period of light before H-hour, which in turn should coincide with three hours before high tide).

The Navy was ordered to set sail for the concentration point on the English Channel and to proceed through the five seaways which had been swept clear of mines. Even in the worst case scenario there was time to order a return to port if the subsequent situation suggested this to be the best option. A second meeting was planned for 4.00 am on the following day, Monday June 5th, 1944.

Ike went to bed that day racked with uncertainties. When he woke at 3.30 am on the 5th to attend the meeting, the first thing he did was look out of the window. The scene was appalling: the wind was blowing a gale and rain poured down. But while he was heading to the meeting he noticed that it had stopped raining.

The weather dominated the first part of the meeting. The news was good: the weather was set to improve slightly. Ike listened in silence, thought for a moment, and then rose and spoke "OK, boys. We have no other option. We leave on Tuesday."[15] The whole of the assault force, consisting of 176,000 men and 20,000 vehicles received the order and set off[16].

Leading means deciding and taking decisions. Sometimes you are wrong, and many other times, you are right. The Allies had planned and studied every detail, had worked assiduously for years, and all of a sudden, everything hung on luck… Napoleon said that "luck is not a factor," because luck usually goes hand in hand with work, so you must seek it out and insist. That is the luck of champions and also the luck of great captains: "the winner sees what he hopes for approaching; the loser, what he fears," said Teresa Zabell, Olympic gold medallist in sailing.[17]

In any case, the gloomy weather had an unexpected silver lining. The German commanders relaxed their vigilance at the sight of heavy rain and cloud. On June 4th, the naval command in Paris reported that invasion could not be considered imminent. Naval patrols were cancelled on June 5th due to bad weather, Rommel left for Germany for his wife's birthday and the commanders of the German Seventh Army left their posts to go to Rennes for training exercises.[18] (Map 7.2)

Map 7.2 Normandy Landings and Hitler's Panzer Deployment (1944).

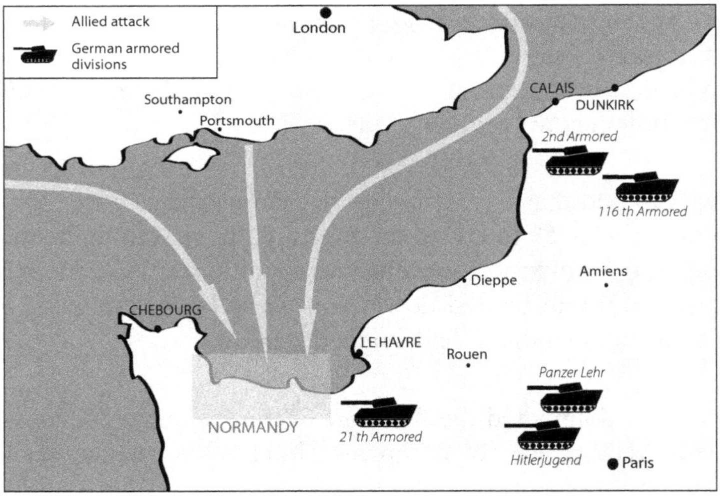

The Germans paid dearly for their lack of weather stations in the Atlantic zone, since their failure to forecast an improvement in weather meant that they would be taken by surprise. But all was far from lost: there was still time to throw the Allies back to sea.

At 10.00 pm on June 5th, the first Allied paratroops were down on French soil in advance of the action of the invasion, for which the official start time was midnight on the 6th. At 3.00 am the *Werhmacht* went on the alert. What was happening was still unclear, but it would not be for long: radar screen revealed the unprecedented air and naval activity ahead of the Allied landing.

By 5.00 am the German soldiers who were the first defences of the vanguard could see what coming upon them. Spread out over a 22 mile front, the Allies were sailing to France in 4,126 landing craft protected by 13,000 aircraft and 702 warships.[19] Despite dogged resistance on the part of the Germans, and apart from a few mishaps (especially on what was known as Omaha beach, where very little happened according to the script), the landings were a success.

But beachheads are very weak and the depth of penetration is measured in feet. It was the moment of greatest danger, since if the armoured divisions should appear on the scene, the defeat of the Allies would be certain.

But the fact was that there was only one *Panzer* division, the 21st, in the whole region. Stationed relatively near (in the vicinity of Paris) were the most fearsome and perfectly prepared armoured divisions, the *Hitlerjugend* and *Panzer* Lehr as part of the strategic reserve. Von Rundstedt gave the order at 3.00 am to move those two divisions towards Normandy. Moving during the night they would get to the beaches unmolested by Allied aviation, and if they arrived at dawn they would be able to annihilate the Allied forces which had already landed.

Yet at 06.00 am Von Rundstedt was reprimanded by the General Staff in the Wolf's Lair, and the divisions received the countermand to stop. Rundstedt was told that he lacked the necessary authority to order both divisions to move to Normandy, only the *Führer* could give orders to the strategic reserve. Thus the two divisions stopped to wait for orders. However, Hitler was sleeping and nobody rushed to wake up Hitler...

And indeed, when the order of keep moving did arrive, it was, surprise, surprise, too late. At 3.00 pm on the 6th, once the morning meeting had finished in the Wolf's Lair, authorisation was received to continue towards the Atlantic coast. But by then it was too late. In daylight the column of tanks became an easy target for Allied aviation, so that all movement was inadvisable. The Germans would have to wait until the 8th for the arrival of the first division and the following day for the second to go into action.

The 21st, meanwhile, the only armoured division in the zone with Rommel in Germany, divided its forced into a serious of partial counter-attacks, all too dispersed to be successful.

Rommel arrived at his combat post on the afternoon of June 6th. By that time 75,215 Britons and 57,050 Americans, plus the airborne divisions, were on French soil. Average penetration into the interior (which according to the route map should have been eight kilometres) was a mere 1,500 yards.[20]

Despite the fact that they had initially been contained, just as Rommel had feared, Allied air and sea power meant that all efforts made by Germans to counter-attack failed because troop and equipment movements could only be made by night; attempting to do so by day was to risk destruction.

On top of this, the Germans were unsure about the real intentions of the Allies, and thought that it might be only a bluffing manoeuvre before an even larger landing. The troops stationed in Calais stayed where they were, and "in some cases the reserves did not go into battle until 6 weeks after D-day".[21]

By June 9th, 326,000 Allied men and 54,000 vehicles had been landed in France.[22] The die was cast.

3. The Sleep of the Just

Adolf Hitler was asleep at the critical moment of the battle (his timetable was very different from that of any other commander involved in the war), yet no-one dared wake him immediately and tell him. The reason? Simply that the circle of his trusted people consisted only of servile fans.

Timetables and health, physical as well as mental, are a very up-to-date matter at the present time in business. Management, middle-management and workers (the infantry in the business world), all work long hours with significant levels of stress, sustained effort and pressure. Yet we only take any notice of our physical or mental health when something serious happens to us, and when this occurs it affects the health of the company as well.

And it is far from uncommon for the managers to give no thought whatsoever to the hours their people are having to work or to their wellbeing or that of their families. The outcome is that the staff fall sick, families are shattered, the environment becomes strained and human resources burn out.

There are two kinds of business – those which allow each individual a specific timetable which matches his capacity for work, which in some cases goes as far as to be completely anarchic; and those which regulate it constantly and tyrannically, exacting the contribution right to the last minute. These decisions appear to arise from no particular objective criterion and are merely a reflection of the management style of each executive (be it their own or inherited).

Great generals exist who barely sleep, who work through the night, keeping impossible hours. Others, no less great, observe very strict timetables, and no matter what happens, they go to bed as regularly as clockwork.

But the experience of the commanders and leaders of the Second World War is this: first, take care of your health. If the hours you work or your responsibilities undermine it, not only will you pay for it, but so will the majority of your forces and your work will be wasted. And in the second place, take care of your team and watch out for their health, both mental and physical, and that will keep you going as well (not to mention keeping you alive).

Eisenhower believed he was immune to common ailments and placed his faith in his iron health. But he was wrong, and he fell sick in the middle of the battle for Tunisia. He then came to realise that "there are certain limits of physical stamina which cannot safely be exceeded without cost (… and that) perfect health is an essential condition for a lucky commander."[23]

But iron physical health means nothing in the absence of good mental hygiene, which in many cases means the difference between success and failure.

Hitler hardly left Germany throughout the entire war. At the start of the invasion of the Soviet Union he shut himself up in his Wolf's Lair, and scarcely went out at all, except for very brief intervals, for three long years. When he finally did leave it, he did so "like a drowned man in a drowned country."[24]

Described as a cross between a monastery and a concentration camp, life at the Wolf's Lair was gloomy. It was located in a dense forest, consisting of a serial of air-raid shelters with north-facing windows to avoid the sun, with barracks surrounded by minefields and barbed wire. It was dank and hot in summer, and infested by mosquitoes, and cold in winter.[25]

In this atmosphere, Hitler and his people lost contact with the real world. They lived in their isolated corner, unaware of the situation on the front, of the cities devastated by bombing, of the hospitals choked with the wounded. Neither he nor anyone in his immediate circle possessed any direct information about the situation,[26] and what was worse, they refused to have it. Whenever Hitler received in his headquarters a visit from elsewhere, his circle were keen to ensure that the message delivered would meet with Hitler's approval. And if that was not possible, efforts were made to sweeten the news so that it would not irritate the *Führer*.

It made little difference if he was in Berlin or his house in Bavaria – it was always the same circle of people keeping to the same routine, and even the routine was perverse.

He rose at 10.00 am, had breakfast in bed and found out what the international situation was by means of a press summary. Around midday he had the first daily meeting where his subordinates debriefed a global report. It was during this session, which usually lasted until 2.00 pm, when an initial analysis of the military situation would be made.

At that time, usually alone, in his barracks, he would lunch, always in the same place, with his back to the wall, keeping strictly to his vegetarian diet. Afterwards he might have a short stroll, almost always alone, playing for a while with his dog, Blondie.

The first hour of the afternoon was set aside for non-military matters. At 5.00 pm he stopped for tea; and an hour later the second of the military meetings began.

Dinner was at 7.30 pm and usually lasted two hours. This was followed by films. The final event of the day was a meeting with his team and guests for tea, a gathering which was usually occupied by long monologues by the *Führer*, that lasted beyond midnight. Sometimes it might be broad daylight when he closed his discussions and went to bed,[27] although usually it would be a little after two in the morning.

Such was his life, with little variation, day after day, month after month, year after year, slowly becoming ever more turned in on himself and his group of cronies. When he left the Wolf's Lair, he was like an old man, looking twenty years older than his real age.

How could he be expected to take sensible, balanced decisions in this atmosphere? To make matters worse, his personal medical adviser since 1936, Dr. Theodor Morell, had been prescribing a combination of sleeping pills to help him sleep and stimulants for when he woke.[28]

What we do know is that of the great leaders of the Second World War, only Hitler was austere, abstemious, celibate and with no family life. He alone had a life of terrible monotony.[29]

Churchill could not have been less like him. Apart from the fact that he was already 65 years of age when he took over the government in 1940, during the first four years of the war he covered no less that 150,000 kilometres, spending 30 days at sea and fourteen in the air.[30] He loved to eat and drink well. He was innately curious about things.

We have mentioned the fact that one faithful mainstay of management is what American business management guru Tom Peters would call the technology of the obvious: he never tired of visiting the factories, the front, the Allies (in Moscow or Washington), the ships of the navy, the locations which had been devastated by bombing, and so on.

When he did once fall ill during the conflict he merely followed the advice of his doctors and used the time to paint and read, calmly waiting until the completion of his convalescence. Nothing happened, the war was not lost and he was able to carry on after a few days; this was why he had his team of co-workers.

In short, have fun in your command. Don't always run at a break-neck pace. Take leave when you have earned it: spend time with your families.[31] And make sure your team also has a good balance in their lives.

4. Paris… next stop Berlin?

Once the German counter-attacks had been repelled, the Allies began to advance slowly but surely, consolidating their positions. The port of Cherbourg was taken on June 25th, although work on the damage done by the Germans was not completed until the end of August, so that until then it could not be used as a port.

The Allied advances were limited, but the Germans (at least those in the field) were aware that they had everything to lose in a war of attrition, so Von Rundstedt proposed a withdrawal to the far side of the river Seine. Not only did Hitler veto this, but he fired Von Rundstedt and put General Von Kluge in his place.

German reinforcements kept on trickling in. On June 22nd the Soviets launched a crushing offensive: the Eastern Front collapsed.

On July 20th a bomb went off in Hitler's headquarters, the assassination attempt and subsequent *coup d'état* failed, and the *Führer* escaped unharmed from what was known as Operation Valkyrie. The conspirators and their sympathisers, all members of the German Army, were purged with great cruelty. Rommel was forced to commit suicide because of his possible participation and Von Kluge, seemingly also involved in the conspiracy, killed himself *en route* for Berlin where he was headed to make a statement about the assassination attempt.

And in the meantime the Germans were resisting in France with the strength of desperation and from an obvious position of inferiority

Yet despite the greater quantity of their resources, the Allies were encountering additional difficulties which slowed them down caused by the geography of the area. Breaking through the front was especially complicated, particularly in the American sector because natural hedges grown on embankments of considerable height surrounded the fields. As they tried to cross them, the tanks exposed their non-armoured side, the underneath, so that they were vulnerable to any kind of armour piercing weaponry. They were also unable to beat off attacks because as they mounted the embankments the slope was such that they were unable to use their guns with accuracy. The Germans cunningly waited under camouflage to destroy the tanks, then massacred the infantry, so that progress was slow and costly.

When the solution appeared it was not from an engineer or an expert, but from a mere sergeant who had the bright idea of fitting two steel blades on the front of the tanks so that as they advanced they would scythe their way through the hedges, saving them from having to climb over them. This solved the problem quickly and efficiently.

The fact is that the huge employee base of our companies conceals a vast wealth of creativity and initiative. Making the most of this talent, in the way the American army did, is just a question of management style. If people feel free to express themselves and talk freely with their "officers", without fearing their bosses, the fruits of their inventiveness will benefit one and all.[32]

At last, on August 4th, nearly two months after D-day, the Allies broke the front. On August 15th, the Allies also landed in the south of France and the Germans were forced to withdraw at top speed. Paris fell on August 24th, 1944. The front was in tatters. It was now no longer possible to defend France.

Since June 6th the Germans had lost 500,000 men, 3,000 guns, 1,500 tanks, 2,000 aircraft and 20,000 vehicles of other kinds.[33] The Allies had now twice the number of men, three times as many guns, twenty times as many tanks, and a mere 573 German aircraft were facing some 14,000 Allied aeroplanes (a ratio of almost 25 to 1).[34]

By September 13th the Americans were already at the gates of Aachen and around a hundred kilometres from Cologne. Their most charismatic general, Patton, had covered 500 miles in 25 days (20 miles per day compared with the few feet per day at the start of the offensive). In the north the British took Brussels on September 4th and shortly afterwards the important port of Antwerp.

The road to Berlin seemed open, while the Soviets were advancing with seven league boots on Eastern Europe. Optimism reined among the Allies and everything pointed to a possible end to the war in the same year. And then, all of a sudden, this unstoppable drive melted like a sugar cube in a cup of coffee. Why? The Allies seemed to have forgotten Von Clausewitz' maxim: "no higher and simpler law than that of keeping one's forces concentrated."[35]

Drunk with success, they had let themselves be carried away, and decided to advance on a broad front (trying to advance simultaneously on all sides, instead of concentrating a much greater weight at a single point). The lack of essential resources needed to support such an ambitious objective weakened the advance and the front ground to a halt.

The reason for this shortage of means may well have been political. Both the Americans, advancing through the south, and the British from the north were both simultaneously demanding supplies, and as in so many other cases, the compromise decision adopted (compromise, not consensus) led to more problems than it had initially intended to solve.

The Allied forces were grouped in five armies, so that the situation demanded that one of them, possibly two, should stop while the others advanced. But nothing of the sort took place.

Nor did their generals display too much imagination or resourcefulness… "Allied operations responded with complete pig-headedness, utterly wanting in imagination, in the quest to gain territory, draw lines on the map and eliminate indentations and salients which they felt were unattractive. Their leaders were trying to conquer territory foot by foot, instead of pursuing the goal every general has seek throughout history: concentrating forces so that the enemy's front can be split in two"[36].

Of course, the Allied troops possessed great superiority in materiel, and were relying on this firepower while failing to notice various factors such as the inflexibility of the chain of command at battlefield level. This resulted in officers frequently interpreting orders short-sighted. They carried them out to the letter, but restricted themselves to the letter and not the spirit, demonstrating little initiative and independence of command.

The Allies had created a military machine which was methodical and detailed, but at the cost of being slow and clumsy. They behaved well in defence and attack when plans were made in detail, but when they broke through; they were incapable of injecting speed into their operations because of the rigidity of the command system.

Faced with the prospect of spending the winter stalled before the German front, the British, under General Montgomery, decided to make use of the Allied strategic reserve (fundamentally the First Airborne Corp, consisting of three division of paratroops, two American and one British) with the aim of capturing a series of bridges over the Dutch part of the Rhine in order to use them to penetrate the heart of Germany before the cold weather arrived. The operation, known as Market Garden, basically failed because of poor planning (the plan required the concatenation of an unbroken series of rather unlikely successes) and because of overconfidence, an assumption that the Germans would not resist as they actually did.

But neither were the Americans, in the south, with more conventional strategies and objectives, achieving any better results. By October 1st, and in spite of the complete superiority in material, the reality was that the western front was at a stalemate. The situation was not to improve for the Allies, who made merely timid advances, until December 1944.

But failure was not solely due to Allied mistakes (and mistakes there were), but to the dead stop which was largely brought about by the successes of Germans who deployed along the entire front an improvised defence, with energy and creativity.[37] Where no organised troops were available to face the Allies, improvised units, known as "battle groups" *[Kampftgruppe]* were formed. These units were often able to hold up, or slow down, the Allied advance long enough for more organised units to join the fray and the front could be consolidated once again.

But who were they, these battle groups? Mostly they were troops formed from groups which had been left behind, or incomplete units, cooks, bakers, mechanics and the like, numbering between 100 and 3,000. These teams were multidisciplinary, worked independently (they organised themselves) but had a common goal (to deal with an imminent threat).

This was one big lesson in business administration – because it would seem obvious that organisations which are capable of forming battle groups to tackle situations that are new and dangerous for the company while waiting for reinforcements (needed resources), may actually end up winning the battle. We are advancing into a world where change takes place at a terrifying pace and the mental attitude of our employees is crucial: their sense of duty, ability to adapt, flexibility and capacity for self-sacrifice. What this means is that commitment is essential to face the enemy.

I am quite sure that throughout your career you have met several, if not hundreds, of examples of workers who are trapped in the straight jacket of their jobs and their mental attitudes, clinging to their job definition (or what they think is their job definition) and who refuse to do anything other than what it says in the book (much less to learn something new).

Of course, your company is not the German army – we can't shoot workers or send them to punishment battalions. (No, no we can't). And defending your country is not quite the same as defending the sales forecasts.

But what we can do is pick our workers when they are being recruited. We can study their CV, work out in the interview whether they are open to new ideas and problems, assess their experience, check out whether or not they have been involved in a variety of activities, tried out different pathways and activities in their personal and professional lives. This should give us the measure of their flexibility and their ability to innovate and adapt.

As a general rule a firm hires someone because of what they did up to yesterday, not what they will be able to do after tomorrow (although the likelihood is that what they will be doing after tomorrow is what really matters).

You can train a bright, willing novice in the fundamentals of your business fairly readily, but it is a lot harder to train someone to have integrity, judgement, energy, balance, and the drive to get things done. Good leaders stack in their favour right in the recruitment phase.[38]

In a world which is changing at an ever-increasing speed and which is completely interconnected, being equipped with human resources who are ready to fight and to organise themselves becomes a competitive advantage which increases the chances of success of our organisation exponentially.

So… back to the borders of the Reich in autumn 1944. Aside from the ability of the German Armed Forces themselves, changes in command facilitated the stabilisation of the front. Von Rundstedt came back as Commander-in-Chief and Rommel was replaced by Walther Model, the *Führer*'s fire-fighter.

Model earned this nickname because of his ability to solve situations of serious crisis, which were apparently insoluble. Hitler had a high opinion of Model and actually saw him as representing the type of National Socialist general needed to lead the Army: he was fanatical and inflexible, prepared to demand the maximum sacrifice and effort from everybody, beginning with himself. His career, under Hitler's favour, was meteoric.

The reality was that Model showed himself to be a competent general who had gained Hitler's favour by his dogged straightforward approach with the *Führer*, which Hitler liked. He was often permitted to get away with things that would have been denied the others, and he often worked at his own discretion, taking little notice of the instructions he received.[39]

This meant that Model had carte blanche not to abide too closely by Hitler's wishes and his men were free to indulge in the kind of withdrawal tactics which so displeased the *Führer* (and which were forbidden to other generals). These withdrawals allowed him to win small victories where others would have failed, which increased Hitler's confidence in Model. The virtuous circle was competed when Hitler rewarded these successes with a greater degree of autonomy, which allowed him to win more victories. Indeed, the fact that Model took command of the Western Front was very important to the way it was shored up at the difficult end of 1944.

This points us towards another factor we should think about: the chemistry between subordinate and boss. Logically, just as it is impossible to rely on luck, it is equally inadvisable to depend on this type of chemistry. And yet we have all noticed when proposals made by manager A are rejected and then approved without apparent changes when defended by manager B.

Chemistry matters. The fact that we get on well with whoever it is – the boss, a customer, the shareholders, etc. – means that our plan is going to be approved, that the deal will be closed or that we get a special pat on the back from the company partners. And that chemistry depends on powers and factors which are not associated with straightforward business management or the performance of duties. What can we do about it?

For more than seventy years, books on management have been trying to teach us techniques to answer this question: stimulating empathy, knowing the person we need to convince very well, making well-founded and even better presented proposals, and so on. From the classic by Dale Carnegie, "How to Win Friends and Influence People", to the latest, highly recommendable, "Never Eat Alone", by Keith Ferrazi.

There is no doubt that it is possible to learn this sort of technique, or at least, to polish it. But at the same time, there is no way to avoid the fact that some people have a better predisposition for connecting with others, and some do not. If you lack this kind of sensitivity (don't think you can develop it) then I am afraid there is little you can do other than make your calculations carefully, launch your proposals with passion, maximise your empathy and be yourself.

8

The Russian Steamroller: from Kursk to Berlin

1. Germany after Stalingrad

We had left the Eastern Front in the winter of 1943 (Chapter 4) with the German disaster at Stalingrad and the gaping hole in the German frontline following the defeat of their Italian and Hungarian allies. If the Soviet offensive could manage to take the city Rostov on the Don (some 120 miles to the south-west of Stalingrad), the German troops located to the south would be surrounded, forming a massive pocket of a million men, which would leave the Stalingrad catastrophe in the realms of folk tale.

With this in mind, Stalin threw his reserves, consisting of eight armies, into the attack. At stake was the chance of annihilating the invading army (as had happened to the Napoleonic troops in 1812) and possibly ending the war in that same year with a Soviet entry into Berlin.

But Von Manstein was able to counteract enemy superiority by means of a manoeuvre which forced his enemy to copy his movements and hence to expose his Achilles' heel. As in judo, Germans took advantage of the enemy movement to perform an expert manoeuvre, which left the (much stronger) rival on the floor. As Von Manstein put it, "Stalin wanted to go for broke without exposing himself, our only chance was to challenge him to take a higher risk."[1]

Map 8.1 The Soviet Threat to Germany's Southern Flank (Winter 1943).

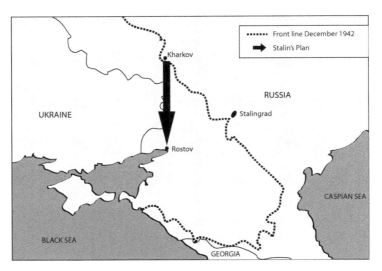

And that was what happened. The slow Russian movement of the huge force towards Rostov left the Russian weak point uncovered so that Von Manstein was able to launch a fierce counter-attack on the city of Kharkov. The Soviets were hit hard and lost a large quantity of men and materiel. The front stabilised with the arrival of the spring and the rain. The Germans had survived the time of greatest danger, and the exhausted Soviets retired to lick their wounds.

With regard to this period, in his memoirs Von Manstein[2] recounts two surprising anecdotes, which have a clear parallel in the world of business. The first was what was known as the "terrific respect for The Russians"[3], which according to him the Romanians suffered from. This fear was nothing more than the idealisation of the enemy, seen as a kind of invincible superman capable of incredible feats and for whom limitless respect was expressed.

Having worked in a wide range of companies in very different sectors, I am forced to admit that, in many cases, *the terrific respect for the Russians* exists in business. When we analyse the competition we allow ourselves to be carried away by this *terrific respect*, assuming that if it is a strong competitor it is because it has better managers and because they work better as a team, that they are more customer-focused, that they use discounts more aggressively and that they always have more resources to throw at the point of maximum effort. The result is that "companies imitate one another in a type of herd behaviour, each assuming their rivals know something they do not."[4]

Make no mistake; we seldom face supermen or super-companies, and what is much more common is that our competitors are capable of nothing that we ourselves cannot equal with work, effort, well-directed resources and a cool head. *The terrific respect for the Russians* is usually – as it is in war – the product of enemy propaganda (or of our competitor's marketing strategy in our case).

So we should avoid allowing the competition to take the credit. In the worst-case scenario it is the members of our own organisation who are responsible for this inferiority complex, which transforms the situation into something really serious. Let's take a look at the case of Erwin Rommel.

While Nazi propaganda had exalted him as a paragon of all the virtues, German as well as National Socialist, it was the British press, which invented the *Desert Fox* nickname. Endowing him with this title shrouded him in the aura of an invincible strategist, attributing qualities and skills to him, which radiated the magic which weakened the British combat morale and forced them to take questionable decisions. One of these decisions was to dismiss a competent general (Auchinleck) to replace him with one who was less able but had a clean record (Montgomery) able to destroy the Desert Fox's reputation of invincibility. In short, it may not be possible to avoid *the terrific respect for the Russians* in your organisation, but at least you can discourage the creation of *Desert Foxes*.

The second anecdote of the period is when Von Manstein talks of the obsession of the German General Staff to create new divisions, instead of appropriately reinforcing the ones which already existed. This decision had a disastrous effect: the existing divisions were weakened by striving to do their work with a shortage of reinforcements, at the same time the new division suffered excessive losses because its troops did not learn until they got into action what older units had mastered long ago. Their losses and lack of experience led them in turn to miss favourable opportunities, and this again caused unnecessary actions to be fought.[5]

The reason given for this was that they did not want to contaminate the new division with the negative experiences of those who had suffered a defeat. Many of the new recruits filled the ranks of the ground forces of the *Luftwaffe* and the *Waffen SS*, units which strove devotedly in support of the Nazi cause and who were committed to the *Fuhrer*'s struggle, unaffected by the conservative spirit of the rest of the Army (that German common sense which had won so many wars in the past).

Anyone reading the preceding paragraph will no doubt be thinking that this is a silly way to fight a war. But just consider whether this is in fact something that happens in a lot of companies. New departments or sections are set up which compete with the ones already in existence, often simply because the current management structure wants its people to be safe from the contamination of the tradition, conservative way of doing things.

The fresh troops are weakened for reasons of no importance and which would have been easy to avoid if the existing teams had been relied on. And people in the old structures also suffer, because they are now short of resources. Thus, more often than not, the same job is done by two different teams.

And the organisation suffers serious losses. Obviously this does not mean the dead, wounded and captured, but personnel who go over to the competition or become trapped in a spiral of low productivity, sowing discord and poor examples among their colleagues, or who simply fall ill. And losses among the veterans are hard to replace in the short term using recruits, never mind how able and well-trained they might be. Innovate as much as you like, but never assume that the problem holding innovation back is the already trained and experienced human resources in your organisation.

The ideal tactic is not to create new divisions imbued with a new spirit but to reinforce existing structures with quality troops. Otherwise it will be our fault that our team suffers unnecessary losses without achieving results. But even worse, we might find that the old and the new divisions devote more time to fight between themselves than to try to do their respective jobs.

When the terrible winter of 1943 was past, Germany had a much better balance sheet than expected and had recovered from the Stalingrad disaster. The Third Reich was strong again and felt that there was no reason why it should not repeat the successes of the two preceding summers. By a supreme effort, over 800,000 men were posted from the *Werhmacht*: "the results of the total mobilisation decreed by the *Werhmacht* from January 1st 1943 are as follows: 290,000 active troops from the latest recruitment drive called up between April and June. Thanks to an extraordinary revision, an increase of 108,000 active soldiers has been added to the entire service. In a similar way 62,000 more have been drafted from garrison and labour services. Transfers between the various *Werhmacht* units and the enlistment of volunteers from the youth section of Nazi party has provided another 95,000 men. Another 57,000 have been raised from other sources… The standard addition of active individuals discharged from hospitals has reached 190,000 during the first three months of this year."[6]

On behalf of German industry Speer delivered over 2,000 armoured vehicles, including the fearsome Tiger and Panther tank models, plus a heavy tank-destroyer, the Elephant. Everything was ready for the *Fuhrer*'s next great roll of the dice, and once again Germany was ready to risk all on one move, its third great summer offensive against the Soviets. The objective: the Kursk salient.

2. Kursk: nobody's plan and everybody's failure

The idea of Operation *Citadel* was hammered out at the end of the winter of 1943, when the Soviets had been left exhausted by Stalingrad and the subsequent offensives.

Despite its victories, the Soviet Army was definitely weakened by the frightful losses from the 1942 and winter 1943 battles. The German strategists calculated that a spring offensive would punish them severely and re-establish their superiority once again. If they were hit hard enough, perhaps there was a possibility of forcing Stalin to sign a peace treaty. In any case it was clear that action must be taken fast: the Allies, having taken Tunisia were now threatening Italy, supplying the USSR with a continuous flow of war material and bombing German cities were constantly increasing in audacity.

There was a protuberance in the front line (the Kursk salient) which penetrated the German front, and it was decided that this would be the best location to strike at the Russians, where they could be attacked from the north and the south of the salient and caught in a death trap. (Map 8.2)

Map 8.2 German offensive over Kursk (Summer 1943).

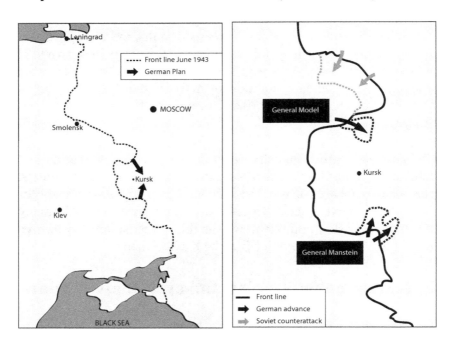

An interesting debate then took place, the kind we have all experienced in our companies. Should we launch the project now, or wait until we are better prepared and have more resources? Should I invest in getting customers, or should I wait until I have acquired a customer base before I invest?

Walther Model, commander of what would be the north wing of the pincer, felt that the troops under his command were not yet strong enough to go into battle with options. He wanted to wait until more reinforcements arrived, along with the new tanks.

Von Manstein, Commander-in-Chief of the armies to attack from the south, was in favour of attacking as soon as possible. With every passing day the Soviets were recovering from their losses in manpower and material, but they were also fortifying the wings of the salient in response to their observation that the enemy was concentrating in the zone.

The operation, which had been decided upon and approved for the first fortnight in May, was delayed again and again. The lack of necessary preparation was automatically blamed, all feeling that they needed a greater number of *'silver bullets'* (in the form of new tanks).

When finally a date was fixed for the operation it turned out that none of the generals had the plan they wanted. It was too late to attack and the new tanks were not sufficiently tested under actual fire. The Russians had lost no time and now were very strong.

Yet again a compromise solution was adopted which was to nobody's liking. It was decided to launch the offensive for those strange reasons which sometimes govern human organisations "since-we-have-come-this-far-we-can't-leave-the-job-half-done-even-though-I-don't-like-it-one-little-bit". The offensive began on July 5th 1943 – six weeks after the spring of the plan!

The Russians were waiting. Thanks to their spies and the Enigma machine they knew of the Germans' intentions almost at the same moment they dreamed it up. They had had six weeks to muster defensive and anti-tank equipment (minefields, rocket launchers, heavy artillery, etc.). They already had over a million men in the zone, with 3,000 tanks and 13,000 guns (almost half of which were anti-tank guns). Their strategic reserve consisted of 500,000 men, 6,000 guns and 1,500 tanks. In addition there were 3,000 aircraft.

On the other side, the Germans had 435,000 men, 10,000 guns, 3,200 tanks and 2,000 aircraft. This was all for a front that was 62 miles long[7] where the element of surprise had been lost. Despite their numerical inferiority, they were confident of their potential and so on July 5th 1943 the German troops went into battle. They managed to advance, albeit very slowly, and losses on both sides were serious.

Moscow was amazed. How could it be that the Germans, despite the fact that we know all about their forces and their preparations, are advancing? With 40% of our army committed to the struggle, what will happen if the Germans achieve their objective?

But the atmosphere was no better in the Wolf's Lair. Model was hardly making any progress in the north, and despite Von Manstein's pincer having managed to advance 30 miles nobody was satisfied with the results. Von Manstein asked for reinforcements with the aim of breaking through the thin barrier that separated him from Model once the main Russian defences had been thrown down.

Events took another turn on July 10th, when the Americans and British disembarked in Sicily. Hitler abandoned his Army on the Eastern Front once again. He ordered advances to be halted, troops to return to their starting positions and reinforcements to be sent to Italy, and these forces had to be found from the Eastern Front. "Anyway, things were not proceeding as we expected", he reasoned. The battle degenerated into a savage struggle of tanks and men which drained both sides, but which (obviously) weakened the weakest side most, the Germans.

As in a poker game, Germany should have raised her bet on beating the Soviets. Staking everything on destroying the Russians (even though it may have exacerbated the risk in Norway, France, Italy or the Balkans), might even have ended the war (or at least it would have given the Germans a chance to seal the Eastern Front and reinforce their position for a counter-offensive in response to the pressure from the Allies on the Western Front). Perhaps the battle of Kursk might have been different having abandoned Tunisia in time. All their trained troops would have been enough to upset the balance in Kursk, and above all to have launched the battle some weeks earlier, and not given the Russians sufficient time to reinforce the salient.

But Hitler was unwilling to sacrifice future success to present risk.[8] It seemed as though Germany, knowing that its cards were bad, was insisting yet again on bluffing, abandoning the game when the bets were too high (weakening its position, since recovering it would demand staking much more on much worse cards).

Despite heavy losses, victory went to the Russians. In the first place they contained the Germans and in the second, their speed in replacing units and men gave them a precious advantage over a weakened German Army which had wasted it valuable armoured units which had been reformed and re-equipped at such cost. The German offensive had led them to a position of clear inferiority, which would prevent them from recovering the initiative on the Eastern Front for the rest of the war. By August on the entire front there were 2,500 German tanks facing 8,000 Soviet tanks.[9]

The keenly awaited '*silver bullets*', the formidable Tigers and Panthers, had not been deployed in sufficient numbers, and they also suffered from some manufacturing faults which were not to be fixed until some time later. The fearsome Elephant, a mammoth armoured tank-destroyer, turned out to be very vulnerable to infantry attack. Betting on that card alone had merely had the effect of strengthening the Russians. The attempted breakthrough by a direct approach had inflicted heavy losses on the enemy, but in the end it was nothing by a noisy failure.

The lesson is clear: never wait for optimum conditions or for your products or services to be perfect... Attack when the enemy is weak!

3. One more year of war

Kursk was the turning point of the war. The Soviets, spurred on by the victory, would begin to re-conquer foot by foot the territory lost by mid-1941, taking advantage of German weakness. Even so, they would take another twelve months to drive them from the USSR once and for all.

After August, the Soviets counter-attacked with significant reserves and drove the German Army back on all fronts in a series of coordinated attacks which little by little broke the back-bone of the *Wehrmacht*.

Even so, fighting was no less fierce. Germany was now simply running out of men and materiel, which had a serious affect on its mobility and compromised its strategy (basically it was only capable of a static, more economic, defence, which could be mounted with less trained and less motorised troops). This static defence was complemented with highly technically equipped and mobile groups, able to counter-attack when necessary.

The problem associated with this tactic was that now they could be easily overtaken and then surrounded, using the same pincer movement which the *Werhmacht* had made so much use of during the initial stage of the war in the USSR. And in fact, this was to be the rule until the end of the war in the East: the Soviets manoeuvring to avoid the German defences and the Germans always fighting so as not to be sealed off.

While the Soviet vehicle pool grew remorselessly, that of the Germans was down by nearly 50% in comparison with the figure it had reach in January 1943. The number of half-track vehicles had fallen from 28,000 units in 1943 to 11,000 by the end of 1944. In this year only 10% of the German army was mechanised.

Under pressure of circumstances the German soldier was becoming used to fighting without a single German aircraft in sight, with dwindling supplies of fuel and munitions, with lorries and combat vehicles short of tyres, spare parts and lubricants, horse-drawn transports and to long marches on foot. There still remained a small nucleus equipped with high quality modern weapons which served to sustain the idea of a modern army; but for the rest the picture was not so very different from the battles of the 1918 front,[10] although the enemy was now very different.

After Kursk, the Red Army gave the Germans no quarter, and they were forced to withdraw again and again, responding by an active defence with occasional counter-attacks, but which lacked the manpower and materiel to hold back the Russian steamroller. Kharkov was liberated in August. Smolensk in September. Kiev was re-conquered in November 1943 (Map 8.3).

Map 8.3 Soviet advances (August 1943-December 1944).

Nor did the winter of 1944 bring any better news for the Germans: in January the siege of Leningrad was lifted (after nearly 900 days of siege), while in the south the Germans lost the whole of Ukraine and Romania was invaded in March.

But even so, although the Germans were losing, time and again they managed to avoid being encircled, fighting with courage, determination and discipline. In March 1944 Von Manstein was relieved of his command of the Southern Group of the German Army and replaced by Walther Model. Then suddenly the front seemed to stabilise, although Odessa (near the border between Ukraine and Moldavia) fell in April and the Crimean Peninsula in May.

Germany was running out of time. A second front had already been opened in France (it was now June 1944) and in the east, having taken a breather to concentrate and reorganise, the Russians were preparing for their version of what Saddam Hussein decades later would call the Mother of All Battles.

4. Stalin at the gates

In June 1944, the USSR was ready to take its long prepared revenge: to drive the Germans from their soil. With Ukraine liberated, it was clear that the next victim would be the central group of German armies at that time occupying a part of the Soviet Union, garrisoning a 450 miles-long front.

The only possibility open to Germany was to withdraw in time, reducing the front and allowing for a greater concentration of her resources. In this way it could save the situation, leaving the Russians with not targets for their mighty vanguard.

If you can't defend it all, it is better to withdraw, reduce the front and successfully defend at least a profitable market segment... At the very least you will buy time. It was Frederick the Great who, almost two hundred years earlier had said: "He who intends to defend everything defends nothing".

The Russians had managed to persuade the Germans to believe that the offensive would be towards the south, from Ukraine, to then swing north and isolate the enemy against the Baltic, or rather to swing south and trap them against the Balkans. This was the idea that Hitler, too, thought sensible, so he ceased to listen to any of his people who disagreed with his intuition. When the Soviet offensive was about to commence, the Germans reinforced the southern group of armies, ignoring the concentration of forces facing the army of the centre.

In any case, and as often happens in business, Hitler had no advisers prepared to criticise the ideas of the CEO. The job of these advisers (or rather, non-advisers) was to waste no time in saying what their leader wanted to hear, even though this might have been the diametrical opposite of what they ought to say.

On June 22th, the date of the third anniversary of the German invasion, Operation Bagration was launched (in honour of the Russian general

Piotr Bagration who died at the battle of Borodino facing Napoleon's army). Nearly two million men, with 6,000 tanks, 24,000 pieces of artillery and over 6,000 aircraft set out to annihilate the invading enemy. Facing them, the *Werhmacht* had hardly 800,000 men, 600 tanks, 9,500 guns of all kinds and less than 900 aircraft. The disaster was inevitable and the front collapsed.

What had been possible in 1943 had turned into unreachable dream in 1944. The *Luftwaffe* failed to appear because it had been utterly driven from the skies of the Reich, striving to defend the cities and factories from Allied bombing. Nor was any strategic reserve available, which until then had consisted of the troops stationed in France, because now it was a haemorrhage on the Western Front too.

The Soviet infantry had sufficient lorries and all-terrain vehicles to follow the armoured units and exploit the breaches opened up in the German positions. Their materiel was not only of Soviet origin, as a significant percentage came from American and British factories. The value of the coalition was finally being displayed in its totality.

In June 1944 the fortified cities were surrounded and devastated. There were no more reserves to fill the cracks in the front, and the units (lacking mobility) were unable to withdraw fast enough and became cannon fodder for the Soviet Air Force which flattened any concentration of mobile German units free of any air opposition.

The Germans lost 25 divisions (some 350,000 men) in a catastrophe of greater proportions than the fall of Stalingrad.[11] The Russians liberated all of their soil and penetrated 250 miles into German-held territory. The gates to Poland were open. Capturing Warsaw and taking the Vistula River, the plains of Europe which led straight to Berlin awaited the Soviet advance.

In August, with Stalin at the gates of Warsaw, the Poles rose against the Germans. After six years of Nazi occupation the prospect of replacing this with the Communist yoke was less than cheerful, so they worked out that if they were able to liberate their capital they would have a seat at the negotiating table after the collapse of the Germans.[12] What they did not know was that *Uncle Joe* Stalin was in no hurry or mood to support the Poles. So he halted his troops and waited quietly. After three and a half months of non-stop advance, the rest was a balm of ease for the Soviet soldiers.

But even worse for the Poles, he showed no interest in supporting the Allies who indeed had attempted by any means to help the Poles, sending food, weapons and munitions by air. Aircraft taking off from Great Britain and Italy were not even permitted to land in Soviet territory to refuel.

The Western Allies were horrified. The war had begun for Polish freedom, and now, despite the fact that hundred of thousands of Poles were battling on all fronts in the Allied and Soviet armies, it seemed as though Stalin was prepared to abide by some sort of agreement with Hitler to leave Polish territory alone. The Americans, and particularly the British, weighed up the decision to send materiel and to suspend war finance for the Russians, but they decided to keep the coalition united because, as Churchill reaffirmed, "sometimes you have to stick with the common cause, never mind how humiliating and awful it may seem".[13] It was a difficult moment, especially for the British Prime Minister, who took the decision with a great deal of pain.

In any case, it was the Poles who bore the brunt. Without support from the outside, they were easily taken by the Germans who massacred then and razed Warsaw to its foundations. Yet in spite of everything, the coalition between Russians and Allies held.

Stalin, with his excellent strategic vision, was already considering the Europe of after the war. He launched a summer offensive in the north, liberating the Baltic states. Finland capitulated and signed a peace treaty with the Russians in September. 260,000 German soldiers were encircled and hence abandoned to their fate in the Latvian region of Kurland, facing the Baltic.

Nor was any quarter given to the Germans in the south. In July, with a superiority of two to one in infantry and nearly three to one in tanks, plus six to one in aircraft, the Soviets launched an attack… The front fell at several points at the same time, and the Romanians and Bulgarians changed sides, opening the front to the Russian attackers. The Germans were helplessly overtaken, and another 17 German divisions were swallowed by the Russian bear, some 380,000 essential men.[14] The Germans initiated an anti-clockwise move to withdraw from the Balkans and Greece. At the last moment they escaped being cut in two.

The Hungarians and Slovaks also attempted to withdraw from the war. The Germans responded by invading them in fury. They resisted with the strength of desperation. In any case, neither was the German situation particularly positive. With Budapest and Vienna in the south; Warsaw, and further on, Berlin in the centre; and Konigsberg and east Prussia to the north within a stone's throw of the Russian tanks, everything seemed to suggest that they would be unable to bear the Soviet thrust for much longer.

All these offensives were made without quarter or rest and smashed the greater part of the German armed forces to smithereens. Even so, there were no victories that were cost-free or easy. The human costs were incalculable, yet the commanders seemed unconcerned as long as the desired final victory was won. In actual fact, this seems to have been the pattern throughout the war, and an indifference to the value of human life seems to have been as much a feature of the decisions taken by the General Staff in Moscow.

In favour of this strategy was the Russian character, with its huge capacity for bearing suffering (as well as inflicting it). The assaults led by their infantry and tanks depended as much on the sacrifice of lives as on any tactical approach, or even common prudence.[15]

Stalin's soldiers were not very highly trained, leaving so many things to improvisation, and they were badly organised and commanded at battlefield level. But they made up for these shortcomings with toughness, courage and a level of determination, which made them unbeatable.

The readiness of the troops to sacrifice themselves was remarkable. If the Russian generals found a minefield protected by German defensive fire, they simply called upon the infantry to advance as if the mines did not exist and to drive the defenders from the field. Once a path had been opened, engineers were called in to clean it and prepare it for the tanks.[16] Neither the Allies nor the Germans displayed such indifference to the value of human life (in their own ranks).

As for the Soviet generals, they had gained enormously. They had learned how to plan and execute operations. They were unscrupulous (with their own men as well), but they also had great talent, exceptional in some cases, often revealing great imagination. As the enemy became weaker, they grew in strength. As Guderian put it, "the Russians became more audacious as they advanced".[17]

In short, the Russian commanders were effective managers with no interest in efficiency. In any other army they would not have won the victories they did because their men would simply have walked away from such sacrifices and privations. The Russian generals were like those one-up men we often meet in our organisations, who understand that the end justifies the means, yet they were by no means incompetent, and those who failed to cut the mustard were swiftly demoted (and sometimes shot).

Nowadays in Europe this style of leadership, which we could call the '*hitman*' style ("get it done at all costs") is fortunately very much out of favour as a business philosophy, although it is still possible to find cases where it is still in use by some managers.

But in any case, there is no shortage of companies where losses in relation to the results are of little importance. The *hitman*, I'm afraid, still has his place in the business world. If you find yourself surrounded by generals keen on this type of management, make sure that your organisation can tolerate those levels of losses and that your human resources have a level of commitment equal to that of the Russian soldier (or you will find yourself open to a revolt in the form of losses, low productivity and the like).

It is usual for many companies to strive as though they had two armies in the field at the same time. Some managers behave like the Americans: they demand sacrifice only when it is really worthy, they provide themselves with highest possible level of technical means in an effort to keep losses to a minimum; while others work like the Soviets, with no interest in reducing losses or investment in technical methods.

Both the United States and the Soviet Union were decisive in the victory over Germany, but while the cost in the former case was 295,000 lives, the Russians counted their dead between 27 and 47 million[18], and even those figures were diluted and minimised by Stalinism.

Some organisations allow that sort of thing. And despite the fact that this is the absolute opposite of the politically correct, the fact cannot be ignored that it get results. But not always. Sometimes the results are negative, as in 1917 when the Russian Army, instead of advancing on Berlin, collapsed and had to accept a compromise peace according to the terms imposed by the Germans.[19]

In spite of everything and against all odds, in the wake of the disasters of the summer of 1944, Germany managed to survive a moment of maximum danger. The Soviets were halted on all fronts. In the west, both the Americans and the British had stopped. German soil was still intact; rumours that miraculous new weapons were about to be deployed were rife. And besides, Hitler still had an ace up his sleeve.

9

Armageddon

1. The Ardennes revisited

In December 1944 the Americans were preparing to spend a quiet Christmas all along the front. Although the expectations of imminent victory had evaporated, it still seemed obvious that the war could no carry on much longer. The Germans were in a state of collapse, and it was just a question of time before the weather improved so that the coup de grace could be administered to the crumbling *Wehrmacht*.

And yet for some months Germany had been preparing a bitter surprise for the Americans. Their plans had no place for surrender or anything like it: they were about to unleash a winter offensive, in the same place as in 1940 and with the same objective: a sickle movement towards the English Channel.

This was Operation *Watch on the Rhine* [*Wacht am Rhein*, the title of a patriotic German song composed in 1840], whereby the German troops would open a wedge in the American line of defence, would swing towards the north and would capture Antwerp, 80 miles away. If they were successful 37 Allied, British and American divisions would be pinned against the sea, exposing them to another Dunkirk (Map 9.1).

Map 9.1 German Western front offensive (December 1944).

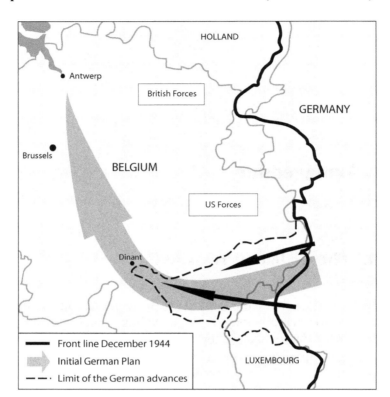

The Germans had gathered two armoured groups in the zone (with no small effort and great secrecy, compromising their position in the east). Although the armoured troops were of good quality, the auxiliary corps were made up of teenagers, older soldiers, sailors, convalescents and Air-force land personnel, lacking in officers, training, weaponry and instruction. All were short of fuel. This was Germany's last card. Hitler was optimistic, thinking that if he could squeeze the western Allies hard enough, perhaps Great Britain would abandon the war.

On December 26th. 200,000 Germans advanced at a 40 miles wide sector held by 80,000 Americans. Surprise and shock were total throughout the American commanders. The bad weather was preventing the Air Force from destroying supply lines and the armoured spearheads of the German advance once they were in the open field.

The Northern Wing of the pincer was moving somewhat slowly, but the Southern Wing was making important advances. On Christmas Eve the German vanguard reached Dinant (in the heart of Belgium, barely 55 miles south of Brussels). An American paratrooper division was surrounded in the important communications hub of Bastogne (40 miles east of Dinant).

Germany was in the middle of an arms race and had made great technical progress. For several months it had been using the V2 missiles to bombard enemy cities (London with particular violence) against which the Allies could do nothing. The Messerschmitt Me 262 was the first jet aircraft to enter the war in the summer of 1944 (new prototypes were soon available). Surface-to-air and air-to-air missiles were under preparation. If the Germans could buy enough time, perhaps, just perhaps, not everything was lost for them.

But on Christmas Day 1944 the Germans had stopped, having run out of fuel and into the Allied response. On the 26th as the sun came out again the Allied fighter-bombers rejoined the fray. The Allied counter-attack began: Bastogne was liberated at the beginning of January. By the middle of the month the Soviets had launched their great winter offensive and it was essential to supply reinforcement to the east, even at the cost of the tiny gains which they had made in the west.

The Germans had spent their last strategic reserve and even though they had inflicted as many casualties on the Allies as they had suffered (some 80,000), they were in a much weaker position than they had begun. The last move of Reich had also turned out badly. Although this time the cards were very, very poor, mainly because of the shortage of resources to sustain the offensive over time, with that kind of a hand, even if they had managed to break through the front, victory would have been partial and trivial.

Now the field was open to the Allies. Their superiority in men was four to one, in tanks eight to one[1], so the offensive, spearheaded by the British, began on February 8th. But paper superiority was not reflected on the battlefield and progress was much slower than had been expected.

The Germans, in their desperate situation, withdrew their first line of defence to the Rhine, to await the final Allied push. The Americans won a key move, and with a little luck were able to take Remagen, a bridgehead on the Rhine some 10 miles south of Bonn, from where they launched a terminal offensive at the heart of Germany.

At the end of March it was the British who crossed the Rhine, over a route further to the north. After breaking through the feeble German defences they advanced on northern Germany, encountering little resistance. In April 1945, Walther Model and the 300,000 men under his command were cut off. The *Führer's Firefighter* committed suicide and his men surrendered. Apart from a handful of resistance fighters made up from combat units, the war in the west was over. The Allies were free to move through Germany (Map 9.2).

Map 9.2 Western Allied invasion of Germany (1945).

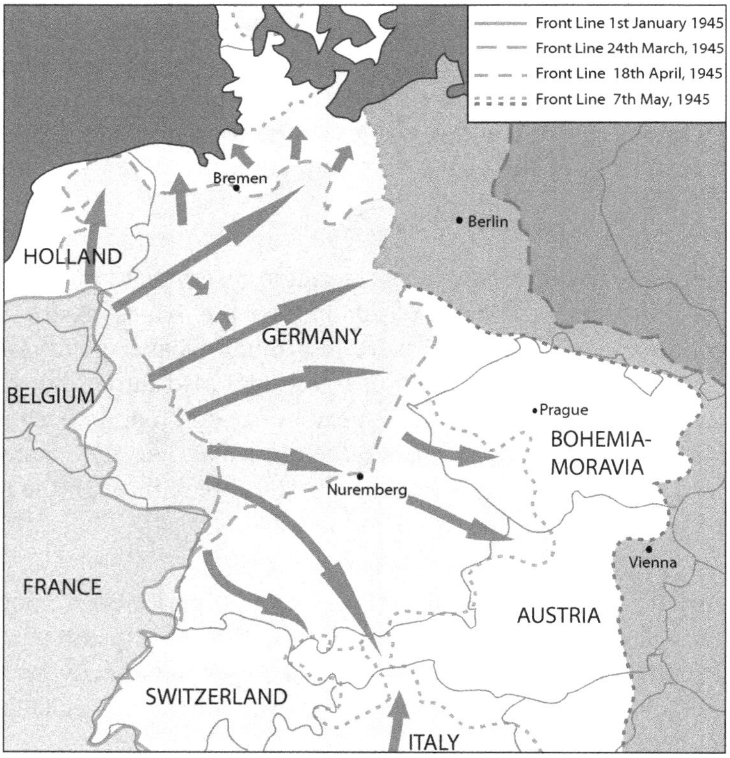

Stalin, however, convinced the Americans to enter into a gentleman's agreement whereby they would stop their progress towards the east. The Soviet leader convinced them of the pointlessness of sacrificing American lives in a war that was over. On April 25th the Americans and Soviets shook hands in the middle of Germany. The end of the Third Reich was at hand, but the Russians intended to end the war in their own way.

2. Germany, year 0

On the Eastern Front, the situation was no less complicated for Germany. On the Baltic a total of some 200,000 men were defending the Kurland peninsula, left there on purpose, when they were urgently needed on other fronts, while in the south Vienna was under threat Budapest surrounded. Stalin was not concealing his ambitions for a new world order which was approaching with the fall of Germany and the end of the war.

And yet the most decisive front extended along the Vistula and Eastern Prussia, where two million Germans, with 4,000 tanks and 2,000 aircraft were facing six million soldiers, 13,000 tanks, 100,000 guns and 15,000 aircraft.[2]

The last strategic reserve had been spent on the Ardennes offensive and the few troops still active were moving to protect Berlin from the Russian advance. Hitler ordered the armoured corps of the SS, which was returning from Belgium to deploy in the vicinity of Budapest[3], despite the fact that German intelligence reports were warning him that the Soviets were massing reserves along the Vistula. The *Führer*'s interpretation that the Vistula was a bluff and that the real objective of the Soviet offensive was Hungary. And even though in reality at that time all German hope was gone, it is a fact that their Commander-in-Chief's mistaken decision yet again made the German catastrophe even worse.

In any case, German morale was in tatters. The soldiers fought with the strength of desperation, aware that the Russians would show no pity or mercy, that the collapse would mean forced labour for most of them, rape and pillage as a matter of course. In this they were quite right, because once the war was over, German industry was dismantled and taken to the Soviet Union, while millions of German men and women were put to work in subhuman conditions. Rapes counted in hundred of thousands, although the fact that no accusations were levelled means that it would not be out of order to raise the figure to millions.

What was motivating the soldiers in the middle of such desperate and hopeless situations? Psychological studies of fighters in combat situations show that in war they will accept sacrifices above and beyond the call of duty. It is probably that the majority act out of discipline (read repression), patriotism and ideals, and so some extent this is true. Others actually simply like it, they come alive in this context.

And yet the majority fight because of *Esprit de Corps,* their feeling of belonging, because of the bonds, which connect them to their comrades, their pride in fighting for a common cause and in working together, in other words, for glory. Their actions are driven more by comradeship than patriotism.

Our companies contain thousands and even millions of cases of employees who work because of desperation or discipline. They do it because they have no option. Where the soldier fights because he knows he will be shot if he fails to obey an order, these workers work because they need the money to eat and/or they can't find a better job. Never expect that these workers will do more than is absolutely required of them ("you are going to be paid, whether you make the effort or not", "They'll never acknowledge it", "It's only work"…). They will more or less do their duty, and some will even work well.

And yet they will never allow you to ask any more of them, to teach them something new, to help them to improve and progress, they will never make any greater effort than is required on the day. Is there anything we can do to change the situations? On the whole, there is. If we act in a way which is somewhat similar to military structures and encourage a sense of belonging (by setting up active operational teams), we can achieve results even in the short term. The members of the team will feel a duty to support their comrades, just as they will be supported if the occasion arises. No more and no less than what Don Peppers calls *Peer Pressure*.[4]

A great advantage business has over armies is that business can select its replacements in a much more satisfactory way, although this may not always be the case. All too often we will observe Human Resources departments striving to achieve the best CVs in terms of training and experience, yet place much less emphasis on assessing how well this individual will fit into the team and into the company, which is almost always much more important.

A well-oiled team, proud of its sense of belonging, will battle on for longer, will do it better and will achieve more. They will face new and pressing problems together, reinforcing mutual trust, which in its turn will express itself as individual initiative in favour of the group. What are the qualities we should try to boost? Loyalty, ethics, honesty and a little bit of motivation. In return we shall accomplish the unbelievable.

When the Soviets attacked the German lines along the Vistula on January 12th 1945, the German structure collapsed like a house of cards. The fortress cities were surrounded and as they advanced on the river Oder (the natural frontier between Poland and Germany), Eastern Prussia and Pomerania were swallowed whole. Some of the troops and people were evacuated by sea in an attempt to lessen the magnitude of the disaster. When March arrived the first Soviet positions had been established on the other side of the River Oder, less than a 60 miles from the final objective: Berlin.

In the meantime Hitler was still wasting time launching his counter-offensive against Hungary in an effort to rescue Budapest from the Russian siege. The only outcome of the attack was to finish off the few remaining German reserves and facilitate the fall of Vienna (April 13th) in a Soviet counter-attack. As Eisenhower was to remark after the war, "We owe a great deal [of our victory] to Hitler".[5]

At the same time as the Russians were taking the Austrian capital, the Soviet troops were furiously hurling themselves upon Berlin: over two million men in 234 divisions and 16 brigades, supported by

6,200 tanks and 7,500 aircraft charged against 50 divisions supported by 300 aircraft.[6] Germany was virtually split in two. There was now hardly any fighting on the Western Front, and the Germans were surrendering to the Allies in their hundreds of thousands. Yet on the Eastern Front, despite the fact that the Germans were short of munitions, heavy weaponry and fuel, the fighting was savage. The Soviets advanced slowly, the numbers of their dead and wounded mounting remorselessly.

The last fortnight of fighting cost the Soviets 304,887 casualties (dead, wounded and missing), and 2,156 tanks, 1,227 guns and 527 aircraft in materiel. Germany lost some 50,000 soldiers (dead and wounded).[7] Such a high price was of little concern to Stalin and his generals. They had won their prize - the capture of Berlin was imminent.

On April 20th Hitler celebrated his birthday. Everybody present knew that the end was near. Those whom the *Führer* throughout the war had thought would be faithful to the end, who had always discredited and conspired against the advisers who had described the situation honestly to Hitler, rushed to abandon their chief. In some cases they even tried to betray him, negotiating with the enemy, as portrayed in Oliver Hirschbiegel's excellent film "Downfall".[8]

By about the 24th Berlin had been surrounded, yet it fought on with the ferocity which both sides were accustomed to, as though the war was not coming to an end, street by street, house by house, floor by floor. By April 30th the troops commanded by general Zhukov were 500 metres from Hitler's bunker (buried 15 metres under the basement of the Reich Chancellery). That day is the day *Führer* shot himself.

The battle for Berlin was still to last until May 2nd, and the fighting until the 6th. On May 9th 1945 Germany surrendered unconditionally. The war in Europe was over, but that was not yet the finale of the Second World War, which was set to drag on throughout the whole summer with great intensity on the other side of the world: in Asia.

10 | The Chrysanthemum versus the Meat Mincer: from Pearl Harbour to Nagasaki

1. Banzai! The Japanese tsunami

Japan is an amazing country which westerners always find disconcerting. However much we know about Japanese culture, it always appears to us to be a land of contrasts and contradictions. Indeed, anyone who has worked with the Japanese always experiences conflicting emotions, and as a rule we go from admiration to amazement in a matter of moments.

Nor did the American commanders deployed in the Pacific escape this feeling of amazement, and they found themselves unable to understand their enemies' behaviour, which on occasions seemed simply crazy. Their confusion was such that in 1944, while the war still raged, they asked anthropologist Ruth Benedict to provide them with a study of the standards and values of Japanese culture (later to become the excellent work "The Chrysanthemum and the Sword").

In precisely the same way as when we are doing business with cultures diametrically opposite to our own, the Allies realised that "we couldn't put ourselves in the minds of the Japanese... Japanese decision making seemed 'irrational' and thus, difficult to predict".[1]

But we should go back to the beginning... What was it that had unleashed the Western Powers in a war against Japan[2] when they were staking everything on their play against Germany in Europe?

For decades Japan had been trying to find a *Place in the Sun* in the Asian Continent, which was occupied and shared among the Western Colonial Empires. At the beginning of the nineteen-thirties, an overarching political position emerged in Japan, stating that this could be reached through a *Greater East Asia Co-Prosperity Sphere*.

This grandiose expression meant nothing other than a kind of confederation of nations under Japanese protection designed to liberate Asia from the Western Powers and which would lead to the development of prosperous societies like Japan itself. In return, *the only thing* this people had to do was to do was subject themselves to the designs of the Japanese Emperor, the Japanese Order, a hierarchy and a *style of management*. It was the same Order and Spirit which had prevented their country from ever being conquered or colonised, and which had led Japan out of poverty and feudalism in a generation.

Apart from its political aspect, subjection to the designs of the Emperor would ensure Japan could obtain the raw materials it needed to break free of any dependence on the Western Powers. Because, although the country was highly industrialised, its greatest weakness was its lack of significant supplies of natural resources.

At the end of 1940, when the main colonial powers in the region were in serious difficulties (France and the Netherlands occupied by the Germans, and Great Britain fighting for survival), Japan saw its business opportunity to implement the *Greater East Asia Co-Prosperity Sphere* (Map 10.1).

And indeed, the United States (controlling the Philippines, Hawaii, the island of Guam and Midway atoll), was the only counterweight to Japan in the region. This rivalry was reflected in American public opinion, which, stirred by the novels of Pearl S. Buck and the stories of the journalists and missionaries, had taken an anti-Japanese turn as a reaction to the brutal invasion of China and the subsequent repression imposed by the Japanese. In mid-1941, when the Japanese seized French Indo-China (Vietnam, Laos and Cambodia, French colonies since 1854), the voice of the people reached the White House. A firm, loud and clear message had to be sent to Japan.

Map 10.1 Asia Pacific 1939.

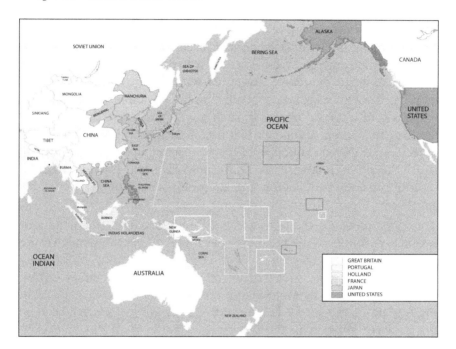

Thus the Americans imposed a strict embargo which drastically cut supplies of oil and iron to Japan. If it were to be deployed to its fullest extent, Japan would be doomed to economic and military stagnation. The outcome was that after a heated debate the imperial Japanese government decided that it would not cave in to American demands, especially as this would condemn the country to absolute collapse.

The threat of the embargo was the perfect excuse, urging them to put their plans into action and occupy their sphere of influence in Asia. Once and for all Japan would have its hands on the necessary natural resources which would make it self-sufficient (oil, rubber, minerals, and the like). The only obstacle of any significance was the port known as Pearl Harbor (Hawaii) where the United State pacific fleet was based.

The Japanese were well aware of the fact that their enemies were, in the long run, much stronger than them, and while both British and Americans could launch a direct attack on Japan, the converse was frankly absurd. The result was that they pinned their hopes on merely a limited victory.

The situation was not new. In its two previous wars (with China in 1894 and Russia in 1904) Japan had faced a similar problem, and in both cases had emerged victorious. How had it come about that Japan had managed to overcome countries with capacities much greater than its own? Success had depended on the principle of its ability to make use of its naval power in such a way as to avoid a prolonged conflict. Its supremacy meant that it could capture limited territorial objectives and then challenge its enemy to re-conquer them, knowing that it would be unable to do so because its naval power would be inferior once the fleet had been destroyed in a *decisive battle*.[3]

This time, however, the fight was not for a piece of territory more or less in the vicinity of the Japanese coast but for something much more ambitious (Pearl Harbor was over 1850 miles away). Technology played a crucial part, since it meant an attack could be launched from a position as much as more than a hundred miles distant, located in the middle of the sea… The aircraft on the aircraft-carrier became the decisive weapon in the war in the Pacific from day one. And heading the Japanese Navy was a champion of the aircraft-carrier, an innovator called Isoroku Yamamoto.

But the innovator had to tackle the experts, who supported more conventional naval warfare, based on gunnery and battleships. Yamamoto was quite clear in his own mind from the start that the success of the Japanese navy would only occur through seaborne aircraft. For this reason his naval pilots underwent lengthy and careful training, while Japanese industry developed the best seaborne aircraft in the world.

Yamamoto had lived in the USA for years, and he knew America's strength. Aware that any victory over such a formidable rival would only last for a limited period of time, he thought that if the damage inflicted were sufficient, Japan might be able to negotiate an advantageous peace. He may have been one of the very few Japanese who really understood the power of the enemy they faced, and as a consequence, one of the few who realised that defeat was a real possibility.

As a general rule, Japanese experts considered that their main advantage over the enemy, apart from any superiority in technology or weaponry, was the Japanese Spirit [*Nippon Seishin*], something, which also had the added value that it could not be copied.

The image the Japanese had of the Americans was that they were opulent, corrupt, decadent and weak-spirited, a picture which underestimated their military and industrial potential and their moral values.[4] In general, the average Japanese despised westerners, seeing them as lacking in character, discipline, courage and above all fighting spirit.

The Japanese, on the other hand, were highly disciplined and jealous of their hierarchies. They found it all but impossible to criticise anyone who was their superior, never mind how constructive the criticism might be.[5] Their war behaviour was based on complex, obscure plans, full of traps, which could be neither stopped nor changed once they had been launched.

In other words, when things went badly, or when something unexpected happened, as common in war as in business, their response consisted of two extreme reactions, both unthinkable as a first option by a westerner. The most common was to continue with the plan in spite of everything, ignoring the consequences (even when they were awful). And on the other hand, the alternative option was to collapse completely, overwhelmed by the responsibility of having been unable to do their duty.

Even so, the strategy intended to ensure Japanese supremacy was simple. At the end of 1941, it was crucial that the only competition in the region be eliminated. Their masterstroke was therefore to have a decisive battle against the American fleet. Making the most of the element of surprise, without declaring war and while negotiations regarding the American embargo were still in progress, with their seaborne aircraft they would bomb Pearl Harbor. With the US fleet annihilated, the Japanese would occupy the whole of their sphere of influence in Asia and would dare the western powers to try to recover it. It was the same strategy they had used with the Chinese and the Russians, but this time on a much grander scale.

On December 7th 1941, everything looked as though it would be a quiet Sunday in Pearl Harbor. But dawn had hardly broken when Japanese aircraft appeared over the horizon of the naval base. The attack was devastating. The masterstroke, *the decisive battle*, had gone according to plan.

The operation was a success for the Japanese. The bombed vessels were destroyed or seriously damaged. And yet luck was on the side of the Americans: none of their three aircraft-carriers from the Pacific fleet happened to be in the port at the time of the attack.

With the first stage completed as planned, a war very much like the blitzkrieg was unleashed throughout the whole of South-East Asia. The Americans, the Britons and the Dutch bit the dust. In twelve weeks Hong Kong, Malaysia, Singapore, Indonesia, the Philippines and a multitude of Pacific islands had been conquered. This had all been accomplished using just twelve divisions and at the cost of three small destroyers.[6]

After these new conquests, Japan was provided with all the natural and human resources it could possibly need to sustain a war indefinitely. The American fleet in the Pacific may not have been utterly destroyed, but even so, things were going as planned.

As a preparation for counter-attacks a network of air bases was set up in the new possessions, in which each node was separated from the next by just the right distance. Each fresh advance, each new island became another node in the network. The idea underpinning this strategy was that each node would defend itself from each attack using its own air defences and those of the neighbouring nodes. Within this network, the Japanese fleet would operate as a mobile attack force which, covered by the aircraft from the islands, would be able to launch energetic counter-attacks against enemy naval forces. In other words, it was the naval version of the system adopted by the Germans in Russia, with its hedgehogs, or fortress cities, and the armoured columns supporting the defence.[7]

Strangely, just as Hitler was unsure as to what to do after the fall of France, surprised by his own success, the Japanese General Staff was also nonplussed by its triumph. "Now what?" the Chief-of-Staff of the Combined Japanese Fleet wondered.[8] (Map 10.2).

Map 10.2 Japanese Conquests 1941-1942.

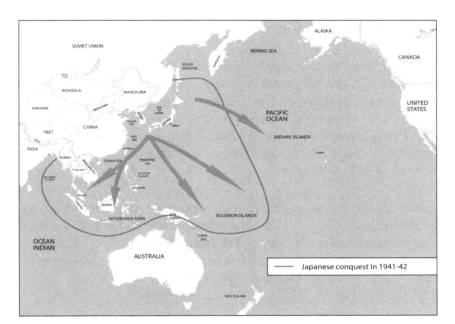

Rivalry between the Navy and the Army made the situation more problematic. No real unity of command existed. The Imperial General Headquarters reported directly to the Emperor himself, although he never interfered in the running of the war; but neither did he do anything to resolve the rivalry between the Armed Forces factions. As a consequence, there was no consistent strategy.

The Army was more in favour of continuing its war in China, isolating it from Allied supplies which were coming in through Burma, the aim being a complete defeat of the Chinese so that preparations could be suitably made to tackle a hypothetical Soviet threat.

The Navy, however, felt that the priority was to advance towards the south or the west. If they controlled Australia their southern flank would be protected, while driving the British from India would make it possible to link up with the Germans. The Army opposed these plans, arguing a lack of the necessary men and materiel.

A less bold solution was therefore adopted. A series of operations would be undertaken designed to deny the initiative to the Americans, reinforce Japan's strategic position, and by doing so this would lure the remains of the American Pacific fleet to a *decisive battle*, which would break the American will to fight for ever.

The plan was to cut supply lines and communications between Australia and Hawaii by taking the island of New Guinea and the adjacent archipelagos, and by establishing air bases, which would impede a subsequent Allied counter-attack with Australia as a launch pad. In the meantime, the bulk of the fleet would rest and regroup in order to be ready for the decisive battle to take place in the vicinity of an atoll called Midway.

However, the Americans were also making their plans in the face of the new situation. In the first place, since Hitler had declared war on them on the very day of the Japanese attack, they decided to concentrate their resources in the war against Germany, which meant that the Pacific would take lower priority.

This decision, taken with great vision and sang froid, had its strategic as well as its political risks (the danger in Asia seemed more imminent and public opinion was more anti-Japanese than anti-German) but it revealed the ability of the American managers to make analyses covering the long term. American public opinion was demanding the head of Emperor Hirohito (not Hitler's), and wanted to first to settle accounts with the Japanese, and then win the war with the Germans. But America's leaders realised that the most efficient and economic approach was to reverse the order of priorities: first win the war against the Germans and put the Japanese in their place afterwards.

In business we hear a great deal about *listening to the customer, customer focused business, doing what the customer wants…* But all this listening is a waste of time if the situation is not seen in perspective. If Roosevelt had had a marketing department, it would have told him that his customers, that is, his voters, were demanding that priority be given to Japan. This is the same as when Henry Ford pointed out that if he had listened to his customers he would have built a better horse and a buggy, instead of mass-producing the Model T motor car.[9] The customer is always right, but he doesn't always know where right is to be found.

In the second place, returning to the war in the Pacific, the Americans made great efforts to coordinate with the British, and to a lesser extent, with the Russians. Despite internal rivalries, they agreed that it would be general Marshall who would be in command: a single head and a single program, while their rivals on both fronts were obsessed by a parallel war where neither Japanese nor Germans were prepared to yield an inch to coordinate strategies.

The Allies decided to split the Pacific into two separate theatres. American General Douglas Macarthur would be the supreme commander in the Pacific South-East (more or less from Malaysia to New Guinea) while Admiral Chester Nimitz, also American, would be responsible for the rest of the Pacific Ocean (from New Guinea to the Aleutian Islands, facing the coast of Alaska).

Macarthur was what might be called a media superstar CEO. Somewhat eccentric, ambitious, eloquent, charismatic, brilliant, and above all, a *popular hero*, Macarthur was always worried about his public image, an image that led him to shape American strategy in the Pacific according the picture the media had of him.

Nimitz was a more modest man. He had a great ability to correctly judge a situation and to delegate his most immediate colleagues in a way that got the best from them in the way of talent and experience. He might be seen as an expert who implemented an innovative strategy. His warmth, calmness, courtesy and good manners soon earned him the affection and gratitude of his men. He was cautious, never took decisions in a hurry and had a very sure strategic sense. At a time when the Allied forces in the Pacific were on the ropes, morale was low and mistakes were being made, he was quick to realise that errors of this kind were inevitable, and he was always ready to give an officer a second chance.[10]

Every general and admiral has his own leadership style, with a blend of innate and acquired qualities, shaped by their knowledge, experience and background. And as with managers, they will be assessed and evaluated by their results. The fact is that great generals have lost wars, and mediocre and even incompetent generals have won them.

What makes the difference is doing it the way Nimitz did: treating subordinates with respect, encouraging them to grow as individuals and professionals. This is the real leader, someone who does not just get results but who strengthens the organisation so that should it occur that it loses a battle (or the company finds itself on the day after its own Pearl Harbor), it can pick itself up and fight for victory.

In a world in which the incompetents and the hitmen occupy companies as they did the top levels of the forces in the Second World War, there is no reason for you to wonder whether you possess the qualities needed for leadership, because if they are lacking, they can be acquired. The first, and probably the most important decision taken by a good leader is to get the incompetents and the hitmen out of the positions of responsibility.

Like Nimitz or Eisenhower, neither do you have to be an innovator, although it helps if you are, of course. What matters is to believe in your forces, in your team, to communicate enthusiasm, to correctly analyse the information you possess and to act in the light of it.

2. Midway (or how to lose a war in five minutes)

The United States soon began to give Japan hints that they were betting on a very risky game. On April 18th 1942 American aircraft bombed Tokyo from an aircraft-carrier. The country was stunned - nobody believed that an attack of that nature was possible.

In May the Japanese attempt to conquer New Guinea was overturned in what was known as the battle of the Coral Sea, which, although it ended in a stalemate, was the first Japanese withdrawal of the war.

But Japan was not disheartened, and waged everything on the next decisive battle where they planned to destroy the three American aircraft carriers still fighting. This battle was to take place in the region of Midway Island (an atoll some 5 miles wide with a tiny port and an airport, the most western American defensive point, and one which the Japanese would have to take if they wanted to attack Hawaii).

On this occasion the Japanese Top Management had prepared a minutely detailed plan, full of traps, for their decisive victory [*kantai kessen*]. This was a complex operation with very carefully timed stages requiring very strict synchronisation, with the weakness that it allowed very little margin to respond to any contingency. Triumph depended on a successive series of events, which had to take place in a set order.

The plan consisted of dividing the Japanese fleet into five forces. The first would act as a submarine advanced party (Force One). Force Two would make a feint attack to the north, towards the Aleutian Islands, confusing the Americans and forcing them to split their forces. Force Three would be responsible for capturing the island of Midway, the apparent objective of the operation.

Force Four, consisting of the elite of the Japanese Navy, and made up of four heavy aircraft carriers, would be responsible for destroying the defences of the island by means of a concentrated bombardment. In command was admiral Chuichi Nagumo.

Another part of the fleet, Force Five, with the bulk of the battleships and cruisers, would remain somewhat in rear, awaiting the reaction of the Americans, who were certain, at least according to the Japanese plan, to order their aircraft carriers to defend Midway from their base in Hawaii and which would then be overwhelmed by a combination of the aircraft from Force Four and the guns of Force Five.

Apart from the complexity and the fact that the forces were scattered, the Japanese plan left admiral Nagumo uncertain about the nature of the mission. When the American aircraft carriers appeared, what would their priority be? To support the landing on the island or to destroy the enemy aircraft carriers?

Unfortunately for the Japanese Navy, with frightening ease the Americans dismantled the highly complicated Japanese plans: they deciphered the Japanese navy's transmission code, JN-25.

Because while the brilliant experts of the Japanese Navy General Staff were discussing the most arcane tricks, planning the best way to deceive the Americans, the encryption and security of the wireless transmission codes had been neglected (the main weakness of JN-25 was human error, as no coding machines existed and the whole thing had to be done manually). It was as simple as that. The Americans were reading the messages of the Japanese fleet in real time and were ahead of every movement.

On June 4th 1942, Admiral Nagumo gave the order for the aircraft of his Force Four to attack the island of Midway. At 4.30 am his aeroplanes were already headed for the island. The first wave was a success, significantly damaging the defences of the island and also shooting down all enemy aircraft, which took off from Midway with the intention of attacking the Japanese aircraft carriers. With the first wave completed, the Japanese pilots who were returning to base communicated at 7.00 am that a fresh attack was now needed to properly finish the job.[11]

From a Japanese perspective, everything seemed to suggest that, as had been predicted, the Americans had been taken by surprise, and would now order their aircraft carriers in Pearl Harbor, now completely refurbished as the main base in the Pacific, to sail towards Midway.

The Japanese aircraft returned to their carrier bases and began to re-arm and take on fresh supplies for a second wave over Midway. After that final wave, Force Three would then capture the island; while Force Four and Force Five were patiently waiting for the arrival of the American fleet to start the decisive attack which would lead them to victory.

However, Nimitz was lying in wait, his vessels not moored in Pearl Harbor, but in ambush in the waters of Midway. He knew the Japanese plans, and although his technical and materiel position was inferior, he had concentrated his forces at the point of maximum application of force.

At 7.28 am Nagumo received the first reports from his reconnaissance seaplanes: American ships had been sighted… He was surprised by how soon the Americans had appeared and asked whether there were aircraft-carriers among them. The answer was no, so he heaved a sigh of relief, and ordered the rearming and supply work to continue in preparation for the second lethal wave over Midway, repulsing the fruitless attacks of the American aircraft based on Midway. "Good fortune will smile on the Emperor, after all", he thought.

At 8.35 am fresh reports came in from the reconnaissance planes. It now seemed that American aircraft-carriers were, in fact, present, at least one, perhaps more… The moment of truth had arrived. Nagumo had to decide what to do: to persist with the attack on Midway or go to chase the American aircraft-carrier which they had just spotted. But if they had sighted only one enemy carrier, where were the others? In the Aleutians? Sailing at full steam from Hawaii?

Nagumo hesitated, losing precious time, with his aircraft on the deck of the aircraft carrier theoretically getting ready to attack Midway, although perhaps the launch would have to be delayed and the bombs replaced by torpedoes to attack the aircraft-carrier (or carriers).

At the moment of maximum vulnerability (with the decks cluttered with aircraft taking on fresh supplies of ammunition and fuel) the aircraft from the three American vessels appeared and attacked Force Four. The majority were shot down by the escort fighters, but some managed to penetrate the defensive screen with a terrible outcome for Japanese interests. In ten minutes and with just ten bombs, Japan had lost the war in the Pacific.

Force Four lost its four aircraft-carriers on June 4th (technically the last to be sunk, the Hiryu, went down in the early morning of the 5th). Even so, they managed to inflict serious damage on one of the American aircraft-carriers which was later sunk by a Japanese submarine from Force One.

The Japanese Navy had lost the offensive initiative. And what was even more serious was that its losses in veteran and trained pilots, as well as ships, were very hard to replace.

On that day Nimitz had only three aircraft-carriers against the Japanese seven, his pilots were not so well trained and his aircraft technically less advanced. But he had a very clear vision of the situation and his plan was simpler, he was able to concentrate better and with greater weight on his objective, on the point of maximum effort.

Is your competition greater and more powerful than you? It doesn't matter, even if the enemy has more means, more resources and is stronger, the battle will be decided at a breaking point at a set moment (in a niche market, in an actual bid, in a certain market, at the time when the customer takes the decision, and so on) and it is then that we have to be stronger and more decisive. Nor should we waste our time trying to confuse our competitor with complex and arcane plans, or involve him in forked-tongue negotiations intended to deceive him. Much more important is to ensure that we have done what we ought to do, like not neglecting our transmission codes. Our customers will thank us almost as much as our Profit & Loss Account.

3. Guadalcanal and Achilles' fury

After Midway, the Japanese made a second attempt as though nothing had happened. They decided to go on the offensive and tried again to isolate Australia from Hawaii. For this purpose they decided to build airfield on one of the Solomon Islands, west of New Guinea. They would thus be able to virtually paralyse naval movements to the North of Australia rendering any American counter-attack from the island-continent practically impossible. A small detachment landed on Guadalcanal, the island they had chosen, and set about building the airfield.

At the same time, the Japanese offensive continued in the island of New Guinea, defended by the Australians and Americans led by Macarthur. On August 7th, the Americans decided to cut off the Japanese offensive at the roots and so they landed in Guadalcanal, where they drove the Japanese out of their airfield and dug themselves firmly in.

At first the American aircraft-carriers were intended to support the landing, but the Navy promptly decided to withdraw them because of the danger of counter-attacks from the Japanese air bases located further to the north. In their place they left a number of cruisers and destroyers to support the Marines.

On the night of August 8th and 9th the Japanese Navy entered the waters of Guadalcanal to supply the Japanese land forces, which were still resisting in some locations on the island. There they came upon the American protection fleet and after a cunning attack sank four of the main American cruisers. The rest of the vessels and the whole of the landing fleet were now at the mercy of the Japanese.

Inexplicably, the Japanese fleet withdrew. What possible reasoning could have led them to throw away such an advantageous situation? Obviously, their purpose in being there was not to destroy the Americans but to carry reinforcements to the island. As a consequence their commander ordered them to complete their mission and withdraw, so as not to place themselves in any more danger than what had been foreseen.

When the sun rose on August 9th, the Marines realised that they had been left alone in a dangerous situation. The fleet which was protecting them, together with the landing craft and 3,000 men who had not yet landed, plus the majority of the munitions and provisions, had fled for fear that the Japanese Navy would come back to finish their work.[12]

Fortunately for the Marines, general Alexander Vandegrift, their commander, far from being daunted, made a virtue of necessity. He refused to become pessimistic and went on the offensive. His men did the best they could to work their way out of such a complicated situation. The supplemented their scanty rations with the roots and berries they could find, they used the weapons and munitions they captured from the Japanese, they made attacks on them to steal their equipment... and above all they did everything they could to get the airfield working, which they called Camp Henderson.[13]

On August 20th they received the excellent news of the landing of the first aircraft. The Japanese fleet would now find it difficult to operate in broad daylight, enemy aircraft would have to give up bombing them without fear of retribution, and in addition they would have air support for their land actions.

In the meantime the Japanese had been receiving reinforcements by sea thanks to the *Tokyo Express*. This was simply a kind of nocturnal men and equipment supply service, which connected the Japanese base in Rabaul with Guadalcanal. They knew they were strong and they doubted the Americans ability to defeat them. Naturally, they assumed that a group which was inferior in numbers and equipment would be unable to resist an attack from their trained and experienced troops, men imbued with the Japanese fighting spirit.

Things were not so easy on the ground, however, and a dirty, hard and grim struggle was developing. The Japanese launched furious frontal attacks on the Americans, suicidal midnight charges based solely on the impetus of the soldiers. In spite of everything, none of their attacks produced any results whatsoever.

While the Japanese were making headlong attacks on the American positions, the Americans were certainly also using their heads in the defence. Against the Japanese resources (adequate training and weaponry, numerical superiority, high morale and a fanatical commitment to the fight) the Americans opposed imagination, determination and an ability to improvise.

On September 20th the first American reinforcements reached Guadalcanal after a month and a half of lonely struggle on the part of the Marines. The battle was to drag on until February 1943, but the outcome was already decided. The balance sheet for the Japanese could hardly have been more depressing in terms of human losses: 1,500 dead Americans against 24,000 Japanese, although on the resources front the situation looked more balanced: two aircraft-carriers, seven cruiser and fourteen US destroyers as against one aircraft-carrier, two battleships, four cruisers and eleven destroyers on the Japanese side.[14] But just as important as the losses was the ability to replace them. And in this matter Japan was slipping helplessly backwards.

Japanese naval pilots were a very scarce elite force. The Japanese navy had entered the war with a relatively small number of naval pilots, some 5,000, and because of the policy of keeping the most expert crewmen on combat missions, very few were available to transmit their experience to the new pilots who were being trained in Japan.[15] The 600 pilots lost at Midway had many years-worth of experience which was lost for ever.

Nor was the situation encouraging on the production side. Japan built 69,888 aircraft and 538 major ships between 1941 and 1945. Over the same period the Americans put 306,180 aircraft and 8,812 large vessels into service.[16] If we concentrate on the aircraft-carriers alone, compared with the 12 produced by the Japanese between December 1941 and June 1944, the Americans were able to launch nearly ten times as many (a total of 117).[17]

In October 1943 the Americans already had 6 aircraft-carriers, which they would raise to 17 by the end of the year. Not only did they have more than Japan, but also they were more powerful, and they now operated technically superior planes with better trained pilots. Japan was about to suffer the fury of the American Achilles wakened from its lethargy by the attack on Pearl Harbor.

The Americans won back all the ground they had lost, reaching Japan itself. They were to decipher the Japanese transmission codes, sink every one of the Japanese ships which came against them, they would be in a position annihilate their merchant fleet and leave the main cities of Japan in flames. But as if that were not enough, they were to kill the main designer of the attack on Pearl Harbor, admiral Yamamoto, by ambushing his aeroplane in mid-air. They were to remove two entire cities from the face of the earth with their atomic bombs…

And this was while still devoting the greater part of their resources to the fight against Germany and supplying immense quantities of materiel to their allies throughout the world (the USSR, Great Britain, China and others).

Japan had rashly underestimated the United States' fighting capacity and the effect that would be produced by the attack on their Pacific base. Doubting, and even ridiculing, the inexhaustible capacity of American Society to reinvent itself and the courage and readiness of the US Armed Forces had certainly cost Japan dear.

In business, as in war, there are two fatal errors: benevolence and a lack of empathy. Being able to see things as your opposite number sees them is also one of the greatest virtues of the good manager. As Robert McNamara, ex-president of Ford, Defence Secretary during the Vietnam War and former World Bank President said, "the single Art of War is the one which allows you to see yourself through the eyes of the enemy"[18].

We are always hearing about the crisis of the American Model, about how other countries will overtake the USA and how American companies will lose their dominance. I find myself somewhat sceptical about this. As long as innovative ability, the commitment to overachieve and the capacity of overcoming problems with honest work and imagination is embedded within US society, I firmly believe that, as in the war, if the Americans have another Pearl Harbor there is no doubt that they will also have their Midway.

4. Great Marianas Turkey Shoot

Japan was now definitely on the defensive. Its only hope was to force the Americans to pay so dearly in lives that they would agree to a compromise peace. To accomplish this they placed their hopes in a series of strongly garrisoned naval air bases, supported by land-based aircraft, unsinkable aircraft-carriers, and the mobility of the fleet.

The Americans, who had secured their two great bases in Hawaii and Australia by the Midway and Guadalcanal victories, decided to attempt (as far as it was possible) an indirect approach. Instead of launching frontal attacks against the Japanese bases and conquering them one by one, a *leapfrog* strategy was adopted.

They would advance in a single direction towards a point where Japan could be defeated, either by strategic bombing or by invasion.[19] To achieve this they would hop from island to island, taking only the really key points (especially those which were lightly fortified), avoiding frontal clashes with the Japanese bases and strongholds (the strategy was rather to isolate them so that without supplies the troops and planes could do nothing but remain idle).

To avoid the Japanese bases they had to create a fleet, to act as a mobile island. It would be an attack base for the Navy and the Marines, but it would also serve as a logistics platform to service them (munitions, fuel, food, etc.).

And it was not long before, in the summer of 1943, the Americans were provided with a fleet capable of performing such amazing duties, consisting of a floating naval base able to transport a landing force to any place in the Pacific and to supply an attack force.

They now put this to work. First the captured the Gilbert and Ellis Islands (a chain of 16 coral atolls and islands between Hawaii and New Guinea) and then the Marshall Islands (some 300 miles north of the Gilberts). In both cases the main Japanese bases were bombed, blockaded and reduced to helplessness. With this new mobility the strong points were avoided at the same time as the enemy's offensive capacity was paralysed. Japanese strategy was utterly obsolete in the face of the Americans' imagination and industrial capacity.

By mid 1944 it was the turn of the Marianas (a small archipelago some 600 miles east of the Philippines), which belonged to Japan (despite the fact that they lay 950 miles south of Japan). In any case, this would be the first time that actual Japanese soil would be attacked. Apart from the patriotic argument, the islands were also of strategic importance: an air base could be built there which would allow the Americans to use heavy bombers to attack Japan. The United States already possessed a bomber with the capacity to carry a huge quantity of bombs and able to deliver that payload from the distance which lay between the Marianas and Japan (the Boeing B-29, able to carry 2,000 pounds of bombs over a radius of 5,600 miles).

On June 15th 1944, while the greater part of the American armed forces were fighting in Europe, a fleet of 535 ships and 127,000 men were ready to land in Saipan, the most important island in the archipelago.[20] Once firmly dug in on land, the Marines faced the *business as usual* routine of the Pacific: fanatical resistance by the Japanese, suicidal charges under cover of night, response from the superior fire power of the Americans and the massacre of brave Japanese soldiers.

Even so, the Japanese saw this landing as the perfect opportunity to engage the bulk of the American Navy and to destroy it in a fresh *decisive battle*. Commanded by a new admiral, Suemu Toyoda who had replaced Yamamoto after his death in the Guadalcanal ambush, the Combined Japanese Fleet set sail for the Marianas. Nine aircraft-carriers supported by 450 aircraft attacked the American fleet which was supporting the landings and had a strength of fifteen aircraft-carriers and some 1,000 aircraft.[21]

American superiority was so great that their pilots christened the event "the Great Marianas Turkey Shoot".[22] Japan lost three carriers and two oil tankers, six vessels were seriously damaged and 400 aircraft were shot down… while the Americans lost 30 aircraft (although more were lost because they ran out fuel).

It was completely obvious that the Americans were now utterly superior in terms of materiel, training and equipment quality. Perhaps admiral Toyoda's only consolation was that that he had managed to save a part of his fleet, which would still have time and the ability to give the all-powerful Americans a surprise.

30 days and 30,000 Japanese later, Saipan had been captured. The American Marines mourned their 3,500 losses, but in return they had captured a base from which they could launch their strategic bombers to attack Japanese cities, and above all, a perfect platform for the next hop in their leapfrog game.

5. Excuse me, what's the quickest way to Tokyo?

The conquest of the Marianas gave rise to a strategic debate about the next forward steps to be taken by the Americans. Japan was the final goal, but the war was not being fought in the Central Pacific alone.

From India, the British were battling the Japanese in Burma. The Chinese were attacking on their own soil, and Macarthur was working from Australia, advancing along the coast of New Guinea, with bitter land battles and amphibious assaults, isolating Japanese garrisons as he went and making his way towards the Philippines.

Nimitz was of the opinion that the shortest way to Japan was to keep on with the frog leaps in the central Pacific and take the islands of Iwo Jima first, and then Okinawa. This would separate Japan from its armies deployed in Burma, Indonesia, Malaysia, south China, the Philippines and Taiwan. It would also cut the supply of raw materials for industry and it would be possible to bomb practically the whole of mainland Japan.

But Macarthur felt that the best option was to swing west from the Marianas and take the Philippines. This would isolate Malaysia and Indonesia as well as Burma from the rest of the Japanese empire, also liberating the Philippines and thus providing an excellent base for subsequent operations (Map 10.3).

Map 10.3 MacArthur vs. Nimitz: US Pacific counter attack (1943-1945).

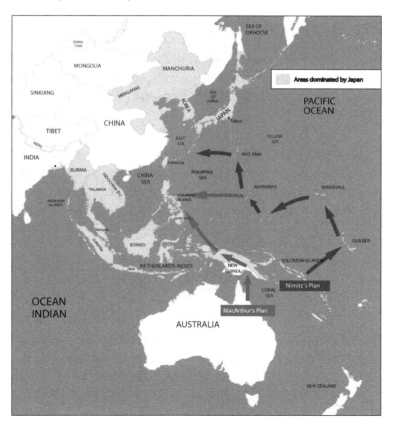

Nimitz thought that the Philippines, with its 7,000 islands and a length of 750 miles from north to south, were a dangerous distraction. A campaign of that magnitude would tie up a large quantity of resources for a considerable period of time.[23] It was also certain that the Japanese would fight for these islands because they possessed hundreds of airfields from which they could launch their airplanes against the American aircraft carriers. His proposal placed less at risk to achieve the same objectives.

Macarthur thought otherwise. For him the conquest of the Philippines was a personal matter, as he had been the American commander in control of the islands when they had been invaded by Japanese troops. Besides, they were strategically connected with his advance from New Guinea.

His argument carried weight because he was more in tune with the spirit of the times and had a very good image in public opinion. Although his personality was much more waspish and egocentric, he looked much more attractive to the mass media. The result was that, with a hefty portion of eloquence, emotion and conviction, he managed to persuade president Roosevelt to support his option, capturing the Philippines.

Of course, I admit it, this is not new… Life is unfair. Managers with greater skills, better qualities, a better strategic vision and less flawed characters are sometimes pushed aside by others who are more ambitious and better skilled at handling their image, at making more noise. Very often, as in this situation, the person who must take the decision is honest and prudent, as was Roosevelt, but who, when it comes to settling disputes, also has his own agenda and will sometimes take the wrong one, opting for the one which he feels will do him least harm.

It is better to be a Macarthur than a Nimitz in the world of business? It depends on a range of factors, but keep one thing in mind. If I had to work for one of them, I would rather serve under Nimitz. And if the business were mine, and I had to choose someone to run it… that, too, would be Nimitz instead of Macarthur.

6. How to get around in Philippines

But regardless of such matters, the Americans still carefully planned their landing, and the Japanese, who were waiting for them, prepared their umpteenth *decisive battle,* as in almost every other case, laden with decoys and traps; and as in almost every other case, with a detailed, complicated plan which depended on nothing going wrong... although it is fair to recall that on this occasion they had no other option than to risk everything on one card.

The aircraft deployed on the Philippines airfields might have been a powerful argument on the Japanese side (backed by seaborne aviation), but in the wake of a series of bombing attacks by the Americans, including China, Taiwan and the Philippines themselves, the Japanese air force was in ruins. On the date of the invasion, the Philippines boasted barely 100 aircraft.[24]

The only card the Japanese had to play was their navy, now reduced to seven battleships, eleven aircraft-carriers (without planes), 20 cruisers, 63 destroyers and 49 submarines. If they lost the Philippines, and with them naval communications with their oil resources in Indonesia and Malaysia, the fleet would be useless, as it would be deprived of fuel.

The Japanese plan was as follows: they would lay a bait, consisting of Force One (four aircraft-carriers, six cruisers and 17 destroyers), to attract the bulk of the American fleet and would draw it as far as possible from the landing area. The American invasion force would thus be undefended, covered only by a relatively minor support fleet.

At that moment, Force Two (five battleships, twelve cruisers, fifteen destroyers) and Force Three (which in turn would split into two independent forces, and which consisted of two battleships, four cruisers and thirteen destroyers) would attack the American landing fleet from two separate directions, one from the north, one from the south, and would destroy it.

The landing would be frustrated, there would be huge American losses for the first time in the war... and it just might undermine the American faith in victory. At the very least, it would allow the Japanese to gain some precious time.

If the plan was to work it would require precise coordination and constant communication between the various forces. The reality was that the Japanese had no overall commander (which meant that each force operated independently, ignorant of the exact location and fate of the others, and failing to communicate its own movements to them).

As for the Americans, they were provided with an Attack Fleet designed to protect the landing force from possible action by the Japanese navy, and a Support Fleet ready to back up the actual landing itself. In all there were 26 aircraft-carriers, 12 battleships, 31 cruisers, 79 destroyers and hundred of smaller vessels (frigates, torpedo boats, amphibious craft, etc.).

The American Achilles' heel was unity of command. The Attack Fleet was commanded by admiral William F. Hasley who reported to Nimitz, while the Suport Fleet was under the command of admiral Thomas Kincaid who reported to Macarthur. Thanks to a direct order from Macarthur, jealously maintaining his independence of command, there was no direct communication between Hasley and Kinkaid.[25]

On October 20th, beneath an impressive seaborne air cover, the Americans landed on the Philippines with the Japanese Navy in alert mode, having been advised by their reconnaissance aircraft, and was sailing in silence in the hope of catching the Americans in their trap.

Almost from the beginning the Japanese plan was doomed to failure. On October 23rd the Americans discovered Force Two, which was attacked by the Attack Fleet and a number of submarines. Force Two lost several of its ships, including the flagship Musashi (christened in honour of Miyamoto Musashi, the famous feudal Japanese warrior and author of the martial arts book entitled "The Book of the Five Rings"), from which the commander of the fleet, admiral Kurita, had to be rescued.

Force Three had also been discovered, sailing to the south of the beachhead. Kincaid decided to deploy against them the bulk of his

Support Fleet, leaving only light cover for the amphibious operations. His reasoning was that this manoeuvre was not in any way dangerous since the north flank was covered by Hasley and his impressive Attack Fleet.

On the next day, the 24th, Hasley's reconnaissance aircraft sighted Force One. It was the Japanese aircraft carriers! The admiral, nicknamed *the Bull*, decided to give battle to Force One. In the afternoon he flung himself full steam ahead in pursuit of the force in question which was sailing far to the north of the beachhead.

But what of the remainder of Force Two? Hasley concluded that as it had been practically neutralised and it may have been withdrawn from the theatre of operations. His target was to achieve what had not been possible in Saipan, covering the amphibious assault and, at the same time, annihilating the whole of the Japanese fleet. This would undoubtedly be the high point of his career.

Nimitz had worked out a system of rotating shifts for his Attack Force so that the admirals in charge would be better rested. Hasley shared his command with admiral Raymond Spruance, who had been in command at the great victories of Midway and Saipan (which had earned him the nickname of *The Electric Brain*). Hasley felt that fortune had evaded him somewhat and that this was a priceless opportunity to display his military genius. Blinded by ambition, he ordered that Kincaid be informed of the new course while he steered his fleet towards the Japanese aircraft carriers.

Things could not have been working better for the Americans. In the early hours of the 25th Force Three was ambushed and destroyed by the bulk of Kincaid's fleet. While this was happening, Hasley's aircraft were hunting down Force One and its aircraft-free aircraft carriers. By 6.50 in the morning Kincaid was on the point of communicating the success of his nocturnal target shooting at the doomed Force Three when he received news that the Japanese had appeared very close to the amphibious landing fleet and were attacking the light defensive force which was supporting them. It was Kurita's Force Two. The Japanese trap had worked…

Kincaid strove desperately to work out where Hasley was, at the same time that he realised he was almost out of ammunition, and that his position (too far to the south) would prevent him from arriving in time to help the landing forces. At 7.04 am he received confirmation that Hasley was not covering the northern flank of the amphibious fleet and was in fact chasing Force One much farther to the north.

The lengthy communication channel, command hierarchies and a series of unclear statements had resulted in the news arriving some hours after the event. Hasley had actually communicated (albeit in a vague and imprecise manner) that he was setting a course for the north in pursuit of Force One. But the command structure meant that the message had to go via Hawaii to Nimitz, then to Macarthur in Australia and only then to Kincaid in the Philippines. The route was the same for routine messages as for urgent ones, and since most messages were sent as urgent, it was hard to pick out those that actually were.

It turned out that Kincaid had failed to grasp the signal because of its imprecision and requested clarification, which in turn had to follow the same path out and back. When it arrived some eight hours had already elapsed. Hasley, positioned away in the north, realised that the aircraft carriers were the bait and not the jackpot. He immediately turned south at full speed, praying that he would not be too late.

Force Two had the American landing fleet at its mercy, and yet Kurita was surprised by the reaction of the slight American forces defending the beachhead. This handful of ships bravely hurled themselves at his squadron and the Japanese responded with a storm of fire. Kurita made the most of his superiority by sinking a number of American ships. It appeared that the Japanese would have it all their own way (Map 10.4).

Yet Kurita hesitated, and inexplicably withdrew... Even today the reasons for this withdrawal are discussed in military academies. Was he afraid he might lose the rest of his vessels? Was he surprised at the violent reaction of the weak American fleet and doubted his own likelihood of success? Perhaps he simply deduced that if the Americans were battling so fiercely it could only mean that reinforcements were about to arrive, so that he would be the victim of his own ambush. Whatever the reason, he lost his vision at the critical moment, when the only chance he had, and Japan had, was to risk everything once and for all.

Map 10.4 Battle of the Philippines Sea (Gulf of Leyte).

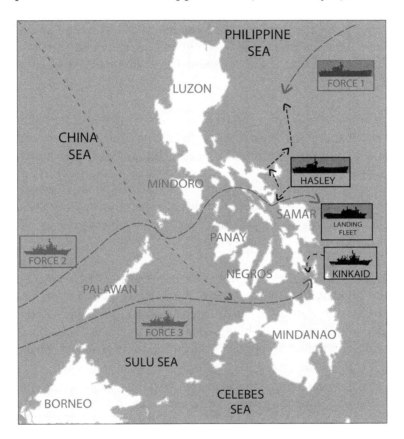

He chose the easier solution. He was tired, he had been forced to abandon his flagship, which had sunk taking with it a number of his closest colleagues, he had been under enormous stress for a long period of constant fighting and shelling. He was disorientated and lost his confidence at the decisive moment, the key instant.

It is true that he saved what remained of Force Two, and that he did so in the nick of time, because Hasley was steaming south at full speed, but it made little difference because the Japanese fleet was so weakened that it could now aspire to nothing and was in such precarious situation that soon it would be unable even to move for want of fuel.

In the meantime, Hasley had abandoned the pursuit of Force One to chase Force Two as fast as he could, just when he had it at his mercy. When he arrived, Kurita was no longer there, so he ended up neither protecting the landing forces, which was his principal mission, nor destroying the bulk of the Japanese Imperial Fleet, which was his ambition.

Vision must be maintained at all costs. Persisting with the plan to the end, not abandoning it when things fail to turn out as they should and we may be just on the brink of success. But how are we to know that it is success and not complete and utter disaster waiting for us around the corner? Obviously, giving a precise answer to this question is very complicated, but I'll stick my neck out and quote the classic of military strategy, Liddell Hart: "Keep your objective in mind and adapt the plan to the circumstances".[26]

We can at least reaffirm the fact that the results of benevolence are usually poor. Withdrawing because mentally you can no longer take the pressure, because you have lost your conviction on the basis of a collection of subjective hints - this is not a reason. This is merely throwing down your weapons in return for some peace of mind.

This also applies to much more prosaic matters, such as when you feel like changing your job because you can't stand the boss or because you're under a lot of pressure. When we abandon a project because it seems nothing but problems, we are often falling for the mistaken belief that it's better to run away and avoid being destroyed by the American fleet, when had we persevered it would have been us who were just about to achieve our goal. As Woody Allen puts it. "90% of success is just showing up".[27]

Even so, the Japanese were severely punished: four aircraft-carriers, three battleships, ten cruisers and nine destroyers were sunk. Nor did the Americans get away scot-free, losing three aircraft carriers and three destroyers[28], some the result of Japan's new secret weapon: the Special Attack Forces, which we shall describe in the next section.

Following the air-sea nightmare known as the battle of the Gulf of Leyte, and once the beachhead had been secured, the struggle for the Philippines was every bit as bloody and long as Nimitz had predicted.

The Japanese resisted fiercly and it was not until June 1945 that the bulk of the Japanese Army was finally defeated. The balance sheet was appalling: 8,000 Americans dead for 190,000 Japanese, losses to which must be added the hundreds of thousands of Filipinos who also died in the operations. Even so, Macarthur got his own way.[29]

7. Japanese geography for beginners: Iwo-Jima, Okinawa, Hiroshima and Nagasaki

In January 1945 Nimitz was given the green light to invade Iwo Jima, an island which would make it possible for the Americans to upgrade the effectiveness of their air attacks on Japan and would provide them with a magnificent base for the subsequent frog leaps.

On February 19 the invasion fleet was prepared. 13,000 marines were ready to land with air, sea and gunnery support of the Pacific fleet. They were faced by an imposing force of 21,000 Japanese perfectly dug in under the command of lieutenant general Tadamichi Kuribayashi. Kuribayashi was an innovator, and he decided to change the tactics the Japanese so far had used until then against the American Marines.

Before Iwo Jima, Japanese generals had displayed nothing more than extraordinary courage and daring. Their courage had no equivalent in strategic intelligence and everything happened with the same sacrifice they demanded of themselves, always ready to die with their men. They tactics, mass attacks, suicidal charges in the dark, based on their valour, discipline and ability were wasted against American firepower and combat resolution. The Japanese generals had the same management style as the hitman manager, but when used against the Americans, it amounted to suicide.

Kuribayashi was also ready to die with his men on Iwo Jima, but he understood that the best way to fight the Americans was to hide, wait for the enemy, then attack from behind, fighting at close range, to prevent the Americans from being able to make use of their terrible firepower.

So it was that when the marines landed on February 19th they found themselves in a slaughterhouse, and the butchery lasted over a month. The capture of a tiny island barely eight kilometres long turned it into the graveyard of nearly 7,000 Americans and 21,000 Japanese. The Americans were forced to take the Japanese fortifications one by one and by frontal assaults. The courage and determination of the US troops was acknowledged in the form of Congressional Medals of Honour (the highest decoration awarded by the US Congress). One third of the total received in the Second World War were won in this fateful battle. Eventually the island was conquered and immediately both sides felt the effect of the end of the battle.

Until that time the massive air attacks on Japan, which had begun following the fall of Saipan, had produced little success. Conquering Iwo Jima made it possible to neutralise the Japanese fighter defences positioned there as well as the radar station,which gave the Japanese advance warning of the B-29 attacks.

Better still, the B-29s could now be protected by the P51 Mustang fighters when they attacked Japanese territory. In addition the airfield was an excellent refuge for damaged bombers and the island a base for the rescue of aircrews which crashed into the sea.

The Americans strategically bombed Japan with rather more success and infinitely fewer losses than was the case in Germany. They began by concentrating from November 1944 on Japan's aircraft and engine factories, with limited success. The conquering of Iwo Jima was a turning point in that it permitted night-time, low altitude bombing missions in urban zones, while by day they attacked the aircraft factories, the refineries, the arsenals, shipyards, railways and ports.

The results were devastating. 40% of the 66 most important cities were reduced to rubble. 30% of the Japanese population lost their homes and some 330,000 Japanese died. 83% of refinery installations were destroyed, plus 75% of aircraft engine production, and some 15% of the shipyards among other huge losses.[30]

A post-war study acknowledged that, had the bombing missions been focused and planned with the aim of destroying Japanese sea and rail transport it might have forced the Japanese war machine to collapse. As with the bombing of Germany, the overambitious choice of targets significantly reduced the results.

In any case, the indirect strategic bombing strategy (including the dropping of the two atomic bombs on Hiroshima and Nagasaki) was directly responsible for the end of the Second World War in the Pacific. To complement their indirect approach, the Americans declared a submarine blockade of the Japanese archipelago, which was also remarkably successful, and helped to shorten the war and save thousands of lives.

During the war American submarines sank 1,600 Japanese merchant ships, one battleship, eight aircraft-carriers and eleven cruisers with a loss of 52 submarines. This systematic attack had a catastrophic effect on the availability of fuel in Japan. While in 1943 the Japanese merchant navy was in possession of 4.1 million tonnes (not including tankers), by the end of that year it had hardly two million. By September 1944 it had 700,000 tonnes and by December it was only 200,000. By that time merchant traffic between the south of the Japanese possessions and Japan had been virtually cut off and sailing was reduced to coastal navigation.[31]

Even this short sea shipping in Japan waters had been fatally injured by the bombing of the ports, which had also been mined. The blockade had terrible results for the civil population. Millions were dying of starvation and disease. Japanese submarines had to be used to supply the many garrisons, which had been isolated with men and supplies.

As a result of the naval blockade and the continual bombardment, by mid 1945 Japan was on the brink of total exhaustion, not just as regards the war effort, but physically, too.

It is almost impossible to speak of indirect strategy in the case of the Japanese at war. Their generals and admirals acted with little imagination and were continuously overwhelmed by events. Perhaps their worst mistake of all, apart from bombing Pearl Harbor, was to wage a parallel war alongside the Germans, which allowed their enemies to allocate resources with greater freedom and certainty.

Even so, Japan deployed two secret weapons in the Second World War: balloon bombs and the Special Attack Forces. The first were fire balloons which floated across the Pacific with the aim of burning American forests on the West Coast. The second were the Kamikaze suicide pilots who, at the cost of their own lives, inflicted serious damage on the American fleet. In both cases they had no effect on the outcome of the war.

The Kamikaze pilots [literally, *'divine wind'*], took their name from a typhoon which in 1281 had destroyed the Chinese fleet which was threatening to invade Japan. In 1945 it was hoped that the launch of these attacks might give rise to a similar kind of miracle to save them from disaster.

The suicide attacks were also a strangely logical response to a fact that was becoming apparent from 1944 on. Despite frightful losses, Japanese aviation had been able to achieve very, very mediocre results.[32] This would be in keeping with Japanese logic and their strict code of honour, naturally.

Since the enemy was materially superior, the very most had to be got from the *Japanese Spirit*, the competitive advantage that the Americans could neither match nor imitate. The aircraft (especially adapted to the requirements of this type of mission) would take off loaded with bombs and would be piloted by airmen willing to die for their country.

From October 1944 until the end of the war, kamikaze attacks, euphemistically known as Special Attack Forces, managed to sink 45 American vessels (the majority destroyers and none of great tonnage).[33]

220

The main problem was that they could not learn from their mistakes, and it would be difficult to improve tactics since, naturally, no experienced fighters were coming back. Another problem was what that the aircraft did not carry sufficient explosive power to sink the larger vessels. In addition, when the pilots found themselves in the thick of very intense anti-aircraft fire, they would normally attack whatever was handy, afraid of being shot down before they reached an objective. Since the most important vessels were very well protected, the ships they found to hand were the escort destroyers and their unfortunate crews.

In spite of the limited effect on the end result, there is no doubt that their suicidal tactics cause great consternation among the Americans who felt that the war had been proceeding satisfactorily, and that they were being forced to alter their warfare system on the run.

When Iwo Jima was captured, the next frog hop was ready: Okinawa. Located to the south of the Japanese islands, it was the first real piece of Japanese mainland which would be taken by assault by the Americans (both Saipan and Iwo Jima were Japanese soil, but they had no stable civilian population). To achieve their objective, they approached the coast on April 1st 1945 with a fleet of 1,300 vessels, including 40 aircraft-carriers, 18 battleships and 200 destroyers.[34] 180,000 men were ready for the landing.[35]

The Japanese had 85,000 men and a civil defence force of 20,000 volunteers supported by 2,000 kamikaze aircraft and a fleet led by the super-battleship Yamato [Japan, in old Japanese] which arrived at the battle in the knowledge that her fate would be destruction since she had no fuel to return.

It was another massacre. The battle lasted three long months, and while the Americans mourned 12,000 dead, soldiers and marines, and 18 vessels sunk by the kamikaze pilots, the Japanese suffered over 100,000 dead and for the first time surrendered in large numbers as prisoners (some 7,000 men). Also lost were 16 vessels (including the Yamato which went down with its 3,000 men on board and without having fired a single shot throughout the entire war, like its twin, the Mushashi... as sometimes happens with products designed to be, supposedly, best-sellers) – and, of course, 100% of the aircraft used in the kamikaze attacks[36].

Having achieved their first objective on genuinely Japanese soil, the Americans prepared for the next landing, this time in Kyushu, the third largest Japanese island. Their estimates were that they were gambling on a loss of 1,000,000 men as the human cost for the conquest of the archipelago and the subsequent surrender of Tokyo.

As for Japan, the nation was in a critical state: surrounded on all fronts, its people on the brink of starvation and exhaustion. Yet their leaders insisted on their national spirit and were prepared to die along with their people.

There were 2,000,000 men in the Army, 3,000 kamikaze aircraft and 3,000 kamikaze boats. In addition, practically the entire civil population had been mobilised, so that officially the militia had 28,000,000 members (many armed with only sticks and spears).[37] On this basis they hoped that the United States would see reason and negotiate a dignified solution for Japan, since the nation was incapable of entertaining the possibility of a dishonourable unconditional surrender.

All in all, the Japanese had made two mistakes in their calculations. The first was to assume that the Americans would not use every tool they had to avoid a massacre of its own people (including the use of the atomic bomb, a weapon with a destructive capacity unknown until this time, and which was really capable to sending Japan back to the stone age).

The second was the belief that the Soviets would not allow the Americans to establish themselves in Japan. Indeed, they were counting on Russian neutrality and even mediation to bring the conflict to an end. Just like Churchill and Roosevelt before them, the Japanese authorities were also wrong when they thought that they knew *Comrade* Stalin.

On August 8th 1945, confused news arrived at The Imperial General Headquarters in Tokyo. The information said that a single aeroplane

222

had dropped a single bomb which had utterly destroyed the city of Hiroshima. While they were wondering what kind of weapon would be capable of that level of destruction, they learned that the Soviets had declared war on Japan.

The news on the 9th was no better: 1,500 B-29 bombers had flattened Tokyo in the morning and shortly afterwards came reports that the Soviets were invading Japanese territory in China. And the worst was yet to come. A second atomic bomb had fallen on Nagasaki. The Americans seemed to be in possession of the ultimate weapon.

On the 10th Japan accepted all the conditions the Allies had demanded in July in what was known as the Potsdam declaration (the meeting of the leaders of Great Britain, the Soviet Union and the United States at which the post-war world had been designed and at which an ultimatum had been issued to Japan requiring unconditional surrender). The only condition imposed was that the Emperor should remain in his position.

This condition was crucial because it offset the humiliation which surrender would mean to the Japanese people. It is also likely that the devastation of Nagasaki might have been avoided if the Americans had been a little more flexible (which they would probably have agreed to if they had been better acquainted with Japanese psychology).

American intention was to impose unconditional peace, something, which the Japanese could never see as acceptable, not just because it was unconditional, but because the terms were inadmissible for their moral values. Therefore they would lose their pride in themselves as a nation and the Japanese spirit would be unavoidably crippled for all time.

But with the Emperor retained, surrender was no longer unconditional, and with the Emperor guaranteeing continuity as a regent, negotiations proceeded speedily and without surprises. Peace was accepted by almost the entirety of the Japanese people who, overwhelmed by the desperation of their situation, welcomed the American invader almost like an ally. I strongly recommend that you read the final chapter of "The Chrysanthemum and the Sword", which throws much light on the directions taken by Japanese logic, so unlike pragmatic western thought, yet which contains codes as valid as those which guide our ways of thinking.

Very often in our dealings with other companies, especially those in distant countries, we find it difficult to see things through their eyes. We have confidence in our style of negotiation born of earlier experience combined with our way of perceiving reality, unaware that sometimes our opposite sides may see things quite differently. Misunderstandings have sunk more negotiations than financial disagreements. Perhaps sometimes we simply have to retain the figure of the emperor. As American humanist Brian Bowling put it, "Diplomacy gets you out of what tact would have kept out of".

On the 15th Emperor Hirohito announced the capitulation of Japan. On September 2nd, on the battleship USS Missouri (the last ship of her class launched during the war) anchored in Tokyo bay, the surrender became official. The war had ended, exactly six years and one day after Germany invaded Poland back in 1939.

11

In conclusion: a sort of summary

From the end of 1914 until the middle of 1918, during the First World War, the Western Front was locked. None of the generals from any of the parties involved was capable of finding a solution, apart from sending millions of men to the slaughter over the four consecutive years during which no progress was made. One British general even said: "I don't know what to do… this is not war!".[1]

The managers of the countries and armies who fought in the Second World War had studied and analysed the First World War in detail. Many had even taken an active part in its battles. This meant that their initial premise was that they should never repeat the mistakes made by their elders. And yet, despite their determination, that was what they did.

They were unable to escape the influence of what has come to be known as *active inertia.*[2] This is exactly like the situation we find ourselves in when we have bogged our car down in mud, and our natural tendency is to keep pressing the accelerator pedal. Faced with new challenges and situations we end up doing what we always do, insisting with increasing intensity on what worked for us in the past, trapped by our own reticence and arrogance. We hire an expert to increase the speed of the car, but instead of getting us out of the mire, we only sink deeper.

And even worse, still shrouded in the thick fog of war we act blindly, not realising that we are stuck in the mud, ignorant of the reason why we are unable to move forward.

Something similar happened to Germany the moment when it lost the initiative in the war. When the way it had won great victories in the past stopped working, the country was incapable of adapting to the new situation.

The leader, Adolf Hitler, was unable to step back from day-to-day details to see the satellite photograph of reality. Urgent and demanding problems always demanded his attention and devoured his time. Because he was unable to delegate, his workload ballooned and drove him even further from what was actually reality in the quest of the false illusions of reality he strove to believe in. While he laboured with activities at which he was mediocre, he left undone those for which he really had a talent.

His criteria for choosing his advisors (based on a negative selection method) only complicated matters and clouded his judgement still further. Surrounding yourself with yes-men who tell you only what you want to hear is not a very intelligent strategy when you are faced with a crisis situation (nor, in fact is it advisable when things are going well).

The paradox of the situation is that throughout the entire war Germany lacked a single head and a single program to a large extent because of Hitler's management style and the huge concentration of power in his person.

Germany had what Michael Porter would call an *Operational Advantage* on the battlefield. There is no doubt that its troops were of better quality and fought better. Yet it had no consistent overall strategy, one with continuity over time.[3] And because of that shortcoming, it often lost perspective and vision at decisive moments. It ended up relying on luck or abandoning the game when it still could have won.

And, as often happens in the business world, when her competitors were almost able to match its operational efficiency on the battlefield, replacing quality with quantity and imagination, it was finally unable to win.

The British, the Americans and the Soviets obtained an enormous advantage by being able to organise their strategic movements by consensus and work under a single head and a single program. Unlike the parallel wars of Germany, Japan and Italy, the Allies fought in a single conflict, uniting their efforts and optimising shared resources.

Thanks to this coalition, the United States was able to concentrate its efforts against Germany, despite the apparent urgency of the Japanese threat. It was to be in its struggle with the Japanese that American forces were to suffer such terrible setbacks. The Japanese, in any case, made the mistake of assuming that its victories gave them an immovable defensive base. Japanese experts miscalculated American power and believed that they were facing the same situation which had allowed them to overcome the Russians in 1905.

The fact is that possession of a strategy demands tradeoffs. This means taking risks and concentrating resources and efforts, ignoring fleeting opportunities, creating enemies who cannot understand our commitment (or who feel that our decisions are a threat to them) and betting on our good name and our future. We have to do all of this even though we may feel that in doing so we are taking a calculated risk. It also demands that we be prepared to withdraw on occasions, always before it is too late, that we know how to sacrifice objectives without insisting on defending everything.

In the wake of the disasters of the summer of 1941, Stalin realised that in order to save his troops from repeating the same mistakes in 1942 he would have to yield some territory and retire to the Volga, as far as Stalingrad. There he took on the most battle-hardened of the German Armed Forces at the end of the autumn even at the risk of losing the city and even the Caucasus.

When he knew he was strong enough, he decided to counter-attack, surprising his enemy on the least protected flank with an innovative suggestion. He ignored some of his experts, good professionals who were acting in all good faith, who had described the idea of attacking the Romanian troops, hundreds of kilometres from Stalingrad and Paulus' iron fist, as an impossible or unattainable offensive.

The Americans also surprised the Japanese experts when they regained the initiative in the Pacific. They avoided the hedgehog positions and the Japanese naval bases by the indirect approach. Put together, innovation and industrial muscle created a huge amphibious fleet which carefully avoided the Japanese strong points, cut off their supplies, and leapfrogged its way to the island of Honshu, the main island of the Japanese archipelago.

The world of business is not so dangerous as that of war, but it is every bit as complicated. Making complicated things simple is the main job of every good manager, and defining a winning strategy in the time available, setting a common goal so that human and equipment resources can be concentrated at the point of maximum effort at the decisive moment.

The history of the Second World War shows us that we can do all this, while maintaining moral integrity, taking care of our people, minimising losses and also helping our colleagues to grow as professionals.

So out you go, into the battlefield, surround yourself with some innovators, listen to the experts and avoid the incompetents and hitmen. Fight decisively, never lose sight of your real objective and be prepared to achieve it by the indirect approach. Encourage a feeling of belonging, delegate and share responsibilities.

If you do it right, there's no doubt about it: you shall win the war…

Notes

CHAPTER 1

1 Victorias Perdidas [Lost Victories], Erich Von Manstein, page 56-67

2 Batallas Decisivas, [Fatal Decisions], Siegfred Westphal et al, page 20

3 Batallas Decisivas, [Fatal Decisions], Siegfred Westphal et al, page 20

4 http://technologizer.com/2009/11/09/great-tech-quotes/

5 Victorias Perdidas [Lost Victories], Erich Von Manstein, page 43

6 "Briefing Procter&Gamble", The Economist, August 11 2007

7 "Indian Mindscape" presentation, Phillip Kotler, Bombay October 11-12 2004

8 Boosting Corporate Value in Global Business Operations Looking at Honda», Satoshi Aoki, http://www.iist.or.jp/wf/magazine/0544/0544_E.htm

9 Memorias de un soldado[Panzer Leader], Heinz Guderian, page 121.

10 "El Mundo" Magazine, number 144. "El Mundo", October 13th 2006.

11 Victorias Perdidas [Lost Victories], Erich Von Manstein, page 355.

12 Cruzada en Europa [Crusade in Europe], Dwight D. Eisenhower, page 52.

13 Madera de líder [Leadership material], Mario Alonso Puig, page 109.

14 «Freixenet: internacionalización y liderazgo, parte de su código genético», http://www.wharton.universia.net/ , September 22nd, 2004.

15 Freixenet, April 2009.

16 Sobre la psicología de la incompetencia militar, [On The Psychology Of Military Incompetence], Norman Dixon, page 159.

17 Scott Simons http://www.tompeters.com/slides/special.php Try it!, July 24th 2007

18 Historia de la Segunda Guerra Mundial [History of Second World War], *(Vol. III)*, Eddy Bauer, Page 99. Allies registred 105.000 dead and 1.500.000 prisoners.

19 Memorias de la Segunda Guerra Mundial. [An Abridgement of the Six Volumes of "The Second World War"], *(Vol. II)*, Winston Churchill, page 594.

20 Hitler y Churchill, [Hitler and Churchill], Andrew Roberts, page 159.

21 Hitler y Churchill, [Hitler and Churchill], Andrew Roberts, page 164.

22 Cruzada en Europa [Crusade in Europe], Dwight D. Eisenhower, page 78.

23 Hitler y Churchill, [Hitler and Churchill], Andrew Roberts, page 275.

24 Memorias [Inside the Third Reich]Albert Speer, page 340.

25 The Fire: The Bombing of Germany, 1940-1945, Jörg Friedrich, page 69

26 Crónica militar y política de la Segunda Guerra Mundial [II World War], Arrigo Petacco, page 247

27 Memorias de la Segunda Guerra Mundial. [An Abridgement of the Six Volumes of "The Second World War"] *(Vol I)*, Winston Churchill, page 626

CHAPTER 2

1 Historia de la Segunda Guerra Mundial [History of Second World War], *(Vol. III)*, Eddy Bauer, Page 281.

2 A part of France was occupied by the Germans, while the other part had its capital in the city of Vichy under the puppet government of marshal Petain

3 De la Guerra [On War], Carl Von Clausewitz, page 180.

4 Memorias de un soldado[Panzer Leader], Heinz Guderian, page 363.

5 Madera de líder [Leadership material], Mario Alonso Puig, page 107.

6 Historia de la Segunda Guerra Mundial [History of Second World War], *(Vol. III)*, Eddy Bauer, page 297.

7 Madera de líder [Leadership material], Mario Alonso Puig, page 110.

CHAPTER 3

1 Historia de la Segunda Guerra Mundial [History of Second World War], *(Vol. IV)*, Eddy Bauer, page 86.

2 El libro negro del Emprendedor [Little Black Book Of Entrepreneurship], Fernando Trias de Bes, page 164

3 Victorias Perdidas [Lost Victories], Erich Von Manstein, page 228.

4 Hitler 1936-1945: Nemesis, [Spanish Edition] Ian Kershaw, page 413.

5 Not my words, but those of one of the best general I have ever served under.

6 Memorias de un soldado[Panzer Leader], Heinz Guderian, page 165.

7 Carl Von Clausewitz, quoted by Norman Dixon "On The Psychology Of Military Incompetence", page 214.

8 El libro negro del Emprendedor [Little Black Book Of Entrepreneurship], Fernando Trias de Bes, page 99

9 Hitler 1936-1945: Nemesis, [Spanish Edition] Ian Kershaw, page 388.

10 The Dictators, Richard Overy, page 531

11 Cruzada en Europa [Crusade in Europe], Dwight D. Eisenhower, page 245.

12 Why the Allies Won, Richard Overy, page 339.

13 Operation Barbarossa, 1941 Army Group North , Robert Kirchubel, page 40.

14 Victorias Perdidas [Lost Victories], Erich Von Manstein, page 241.

15 "Should you launch a Fighter Brand?", Harvard Business Review, Mark Ritson, October 2009.

16 Operation Barbarossa, 1941 Army Group North , Robert Kirchubel, page 75.

17 Memorias de un soldado[Panzer Leader], Heinz Guderian, page 483

18 Memorias de un soldado[Panzer Leader], Heinz Guderian, page 484-485.

19 Memorias [Inside the Third Reich] Albert Speer, page 424

20 The Economist, June 28 2008, page 16.

21 Moscow 1941: Hitler's First Defeat, Robert Forczyk, pages 25 and 92

22 The Economist, December 1 2007, page 82. Don't know who is SAS? Check their website: www.sas.com.

23 Why the Allies Won, Richard Overy, page, pages 107 and 108

24 Historia de la Segunda Guerra Mundial [History of Second World War], *(Vol II), Eddy Bauer, page 283.*

25 Historia Operación Barbarossa [History of Operation Barbarossa], Álvaro Lozano, page 443.

26 Historia de la Segunda Guerra Mundial [History of Second World War], *(Vol II), Eddy Bauer, page 172.*

CHAPTER 4

1 Hitler 1936-1945: Nemesis, [Spanish Edition] Ian Kershaw, page 505.

2 The Eastern Front 1941-1945, Geoffrey Jukes, page 40.

3 Stalingrad 1942, Peter Antill, page 39.

4 The Economist Technology Quarterly, September 5 2009.

5 Hitler 1936-1945: Nemesis, [Spanish Edition] Ian Kershaw, page 523.

6 Stalingrad [Spanish Edition], Anthony Beevor,page 204.

7 Stalingrad [Spanish Edition], Anthony Beevor,page 57.

8 Stalingrad [Spanish Edition], Anthony Beevor,page 211.

9 Stalingrad 1942, Peter Antill, page 39.

10 La caída de los dioses [The fall of the gods], David Solar, page 110.

11 Batallas Decisivas, [Fatal Decisions], Siegfred Westphal et al, page 195.

12 Stalingrad[Spanish Edition], Anthony Beevor, page 247.

13 Batallas decisivas del mundo occidental [Decisive Battles of the Second World War Decisive Battles of the Western World and their influence into History], (Volume III), JFC Fuller, page 603.

14 "What is Strategy", Harvard Business Review, Michael Porter, November - December 1996.

15 La caída de los dioses [The fall of the gods], David Solar, page 114.

CHAPTER 5

1 Batallas decisivas del mundo occidental [Decisive Battles of the Second World War Decisive Battles of the Western World and their influence into History], (Volume III), JFC Fuller, page 541.

2 Batallas decisivas del mundo occidental [Decisive Battles of the Second World War Decisive Battles of the Western World and their influence into History], (Volume III), page 542.

3 Memorias de la Segunda Guerra Mundial. [An Abridgement of the Six Volumes of "The Second World War"] (Volume II), page 286. This pause included Greece, Crete, Singapore and Tobruk.

4 Cruzada en Europa [Crusade in Europe], Dwight D. Eisenhower, page 67.

5 La caída de los dioses [The fall of the gods], David Solar, page 74.

6 Batallas Decisivas, [Fatal Decisions], Siegfred Westphal et al, page 125.

7 Rommel in Retreat, Ken Ford, page 15.

8 "The Launch of New Coke", P. Mohan Chandran, ICFAI Center For Management Research.

9 Memorias de la Segunda Guerra Mundial. [An Abridgement of the Six Volumes of "The Second World War"] (Volume II), page 289.

10 Memorias de la Segunda Guerra Mundial. [An Abridgement of the Six Volumes of "The Second World War"] (Volume II), page 72.

11 El País , March 22 2006.

12 Why the Allies Won, Richard Overy, page 421.

13 Historia de la Segunda Guerra Mundial [History of Second World War], *(Vol IV), Eddy Bauer*, page 189.

14 Why the Allies Won, Richard Overy, page 345.

15 World War II. Behind the Closed Doors, Laurence Rees, page 129.

16 Madera de líder [Leadership Material], Mario Alonso Puig, page 20.

17 Madera de líder [Leadership Material], Mario Alonso Puig, page 33.

18 Why the Allies Won, Richard Overy, page 356.

19 Competitive Advantage: Creating and Sustaining Superior Performance, Michael E. Porter.

20 Cruzada en Europa Crusade in Europe, Dwight Eisenhower, page 15.

21 The Economist, November 7 2009, page 66.

22 Batallas decisivas del mundo occidental [Decisive Battles of the Second World War Decisive Battles of the Western World and their influence into History], (Volume III), JFC Fuller, page 570.

23 Memorias de un soldado[Panzer Leader], Heinz Guderian, page 338.

24 Memorias de la Segunda Guerra Mundial. [An Abridgement of the Six Volumes of "The Second World War"] (Volume II), page 393.

25 Victorias Perdidas [Lost Victories], Erich Von Manstein, page 609.

26 The Economist, April 2008, page 69.

27 Memorias de la Segunda Guerra Mundial. [An Abridgement of the Six Volumes of "The Second World War"] (Volume II), Winston Churchill, page 534.

28 Memorias de la Segunda Guerra Mundial. [An Abridgement of the Six Volumes of "The Second World War"] (Volume II), Winston Churchill, page 419.

29 Strategy, BH Liddell Hart, page 335.

CHAPTER 6

1 Why the Allies Won, Richard Overy, page 361

2 Memorias [Inside the Third Reich] Albert Speer, page 531

3 Why the Allies Won, Richard Overy, page 361

4 Auschwitz, Laurence Rees, page 26

5 Why the Allies Won, Richard Overy, page 268

6 Why the Allies Won, Richard Overy, page 273

7 The Economist, August 16 2008, page 57

8 To find out how it worked, visit http://enigmaco. de/enigma/enigma.swf

9 Why the Allies Won, Richard Overy, page 277

10 Crónica militar y política de la Segunda Guerra Mundial [II World War], Arrigo Petacco, page 528

11 Crónica militar y política de la Segunda Guerra Mundial [II World War], Arrigo Petacco, page 680

12 US Army in World War II. Introduction & Organization, Rich Anderson, www.militaryhistoryonline.com

13 Why the Allies Won, Richard Overy, page 427

14 Rise and Fall of the Great Powers, Paul Kennedy, page 554

15 Mar de Tormenta [Sea of Thunder], Evan Thomas, page 165

16, 17 Madera de líder [Leadership Material], Mario Alonso Puig, page 19

18 Strategy, BH Liddell Hart, page 145

19 Why the Allies Won, Richard Overy, page 78

20 Executive Excellence, September 2009, number 62, page 42. Thomas Edison (1847-1931), famous inventor and businessman

21 La caída de los dioses [The fall of the gods], David Solar, page 284

22 Strange as might sound, many Navy experts opposed the convoy system in the First World War, and if Great Britain had followed their advice, in all probability it would have lost the war

23 Memorias de la Segunda Guerra Mundial. [An Abridgement of the Six Volumes of "The Second World War"] (Volume II), Winston Churchill, page 137

24 Why the Allies Won, Richard Overy, page 95

25 La caída de los dioses [The fall of the gods], David Solar, page 329

26 La caída de los dioses [The fall of the gods], David Solar, page 331 y 337

27 The Fire: The Bombing of Germany, 1940-1945, Jörg Friedrich, page 54

28 Their Finest Hour, Winston Churchill, page 567

29 Why the Allies Won, Richard Overy page 112

30 Why the Allies Won, Richard Overy, page 125

31 Memorias [Inside the Third Reich]Albert Speer, page 505

32 United States Strategic Bombing Survey, Over-all Report (European War). US Secretary of War, page 4

33 Memorias [Inside the Third Reich]Albert Speer, page 518

CHAPTER 7

1 Al McDonald, ex-president of McKinsey, quoted in the presentation by Tom Peters on August 8 2006 www.tompeters.com/slides/uploaded/ Grant NelsonBossidyNEW0811.ppt

2 Cruzada en Europa [Crusade in Europe], Dwight Eisenhower, page 269

3 Madera de líder [Leadership Material], Mario Alonso Puig, page 132

4 Cruzada en Europa [Crusade in Europe], Dwight Eisenhower, page 53

5 Crusade in Europe, Dwight Eisenhower, page 40

6 Crusade in Europe, Dwight Eisenhower, page 126

7 Crusade in Europe, Dwight Eisenhower, page 124

8 Management Review, December 1996: "Powell's 18 leadership principle secrets", Oren Harari.

9 Crusade in Europe, Dwight Eisenhower, page 48

10 Batallas decisivas del mundo occidental [Decisive Battles of the Second World War Decisive Battles of the Western World and their influence into History], (Volume III), JFC Fuller, page 626

11 Memorias de la Segunda Guerra Mundial. [An Abridgement of the Six Volumes of "The Second World War"] (Volume II), Winston Churchill, page 534

12 La caída de los dioses [The fall of the gods], David Solar, page 195

13 Why the Allies Won, Richard Overy, page 156

14 Crónica militar y política de la Segunda Guerra Mundial [II World War], Arrigo Petacco, page 1608

15 Crónica militar y política de la Segunda Guerra Mundial [II World War], Arrigo Petacco, page 1609

16 Memorias de la Segunda Guerra Mundial. [An Abridgement of the Six Volumes of "The Second World War"] (Volume II), page 543

17 Teresa Zabell presentation, 6th Eurogap Marketing Forum, April 2008

18 Why the Allies Won, Richard Overy, page 159

19 Crónica militar y política de la Segunda Guerra Mundial [II World War], Arrigo Petacco, page 1613

20 Crónica militar y política de la Segunda Guerra Mundial [II World War], Arrigo Petacco, page 1625

21 Triumph and Tragedy, Winston Churchill, page 10

22 Batallas decisivas del mundo occidental [Decisive Battles of the Second World War Decisive Battles of the Western World and their influence into History], (Volume III), JFC Fuller, page 635

23 Crusade in Europe, Dwight Eisenhower, page 132

24 Hitler 1936-1945: Nemesis, [Spanish Edition] Ian Kershaw, page 389

25 Hitler 1936-1945: Nemesis, [Spanish Edition] Ian Kershaw, page 389

26 Historia Operación Barbarossa [History of Operation Barbarossa], Álvaro Lozano, page 156

27 Hitler 1936-1945: Nemesis, [Spanish Edition] Ian Kershaw, page 390

28 Historia de la Segunda Guerra Mundial [History of Second World War], *(Vol III), Eddy Bauer, page 259*

29 Hitler y Churchill, [Hitler and Churchill], Andrew Roberts, page 108

30 Hitler y Churchill, [Hitler and Churchill], Andrew Roberts, page 249

31 Management Review, December 1996: "Powell's 18 leadership principle secrets", Oren Harari

32 Cruzada en Europa [Crusade in Europe], Dwight Eisenhower, page 305

33 Batallas decisivas del mundo occidental [Decisive Battles of the Second World War Decisive Battles of the Western World and their influence into History], (Volume III), JFC Fuller, page 647

34 Batallas decisivas del mundo occidental [Decisive Battles of the Second World War Decisive Battles of the Western World and their influence into History], (Volume III), JFC Fuller, page 649.

35 On War, Carl Von Clausewitz, page 147.

36 Armageddon [Armageddon: The Battle for Germany, 1944-1945], Max Hastings, page 165.

37 Armageddon [Armageddon: The Battle for Germany, 1944-1945], Max Hastings, page 59.

38 Management Review, December 1996: "Powell's 18 leadership principle secrets", Oren Harari.

39 Crónica militar y política de la Segunda Guerra Mundial [II World War], Arrigo Petacco, page 1684.

CHAPTER 8

1 Tierra Calcinada [Scorched Earth, Russian-German War 1943-44], Paul Carell, page 212.

2 Lost Victories, Erich Von Manstein.

3 Lost Victories, Erich Von Manstein page 126.

4 "What is Strategy", Harvard Business Review, Michael Porter, November - December 1996.

5 Lost Victories, Erich Von Manstein page 114.

6 Tierra Calcinada [Scorched Earth, Russian-German War 1943-44], Paul Carell, page 126.

7 La caída de los dioses [The fall of the gods], David Solar, page 123.

8 Victorias Perdidas [Lost Victories], Erich Von Manstein, page 600.

9 Why the Allies Won, Richard Overy, page 98.

10 Why the Allies Won, Richard Overy, page 218.

11 Hitler 1936-1945: Nemesis, [Spanish Edition] Ian Kershaw, page 633.

12 Let me take this opportunity to recommend that, should you chance to visit Warsaw, you should not miss the excellent Museum of the Rising of 1944, the Museum Powstania Warszowskiego

13 Memorias de la Segunda Guerra Mundial. [An Abridgement of the Six Volumes of "The Second World War"] (Volume II), page 617.

14 Hitler 1936-1945: Nemesis, [Spanish Edition] Ian Kershaw, page 633.

15 Armageddon [Armageddon: The Battle for Germany, 1944-1945], Max Hastings, page 193.

16 Cruzada en Europa [Crusade in Europe], Dwight D. Eisenhower, page 512.

17 Memorias de un soldado [Panzer Leader], Heinz Guderian, page 451.

18 Historia Operación Barbarossa [History of Operation Barbarossa], Álvaro Lozano, page 442.

19 The Brest-Limovsk Treaty was signed between the Communists and Imperial Germany, following the downfall of the Tsar, the outcome of his disastrous management in the First World War.

CHAPTER 9

1 The Second World War: Northwest Europe 1944-1945, Russell Hart & Stephen Hart, page 52.

2 Armageddon [Armageddon: The Battle for Germany, 1944-1945], Max Hastings, page 223.

3 Berlin - The Downfall 1945, Antony Beevor, page 20.

4 Concept quoted at the conference on "The Power of Customer-Oriented Strategy at the time of Innovation", Madrid November 18 2009. And, yes, as you might imagined, Mr Peppers is another of the world's management gurus (more information on www.peppersandrogersgroup.com).

5 Berlin - The Downfall 1945, Antony Beevor, page 30.

6 Second World War, The Eastern Front 1941-1945, Geoffrey Jukes, page 68.

7 Berlin 1945: End of the Thousand Year Reich, Peter Antill, page 85.

8 A film which ought to be shown in all business schools. If you are a successful manager and you want to know how your faithful advisers might react in a desperate situation, take note and look for similarities…

CHAPTER 10

1 Sea of thunder: four commanders and the last great naval campaign, 1941-1945, Evan Thomas, page 105.

2 By the way, In Japan the Second World War is known as the Great Asian War. If you go to Tokyo please do not skip the Yasukuni Temple in your visit, you will understand a great deal about the Pacific War.

3 Batallas decisivas del mundo occidental [Decisive Battles of the Second World War Decisive Battles of the Western World and their influence into History], (Volume III), JFC Fuller, page 519.

4 Midway 1942: Turning Point in the Pacific, Mark Healy, page 14.

5 Sea of thunder: four commanders and the last great naval campaign, 1941-1945, Evan Thomas, page 105.

6 Why the Allies Won, Richard Overy, page 33.

7 Batallas decisivas del mundo occidental [Decisive Battles of the Second World War Decisive Battles of the Western World and their influence into History], (Volume III), JFC Fuller, page 521.

8 Midway 1942: Turning Point in the Pacific, Mark Healy, page 9.

9 The Economist, October 24 2009, page 70.

10 Leyte Gulf 1944: The World's Greatest Sea Battle, Bernard Ireland, page 12.

11 Midway 1942: Turning Point in the Pacific, Mark Healy, page 57.

12 Great Battles of World War II, John MacDonald, page 75.

13 Great Battles of World War II, John MacDonald, page 75.

14 Great Battles of World War II, John MacDonald, page 75.

15 Midway 1942: Turning Point in the Pacific, Mark Healy, page 39.

16 Why the Allies Won, Richard Overy, page 331.

17 Midway 1942: Turning Point in the Pacific, Mark Healy, page 39.

18 "In Memoriam R.S. McNamara", ABC on Sunday, Sunday Supplement, July 12 2009.

19 Leyte Gulf 1944: The World's Greatest Sea Battle, Bernard Ireland, page 9.

20 Crónica militar y política de la Segunda Guerra Mundial [II World War], Arrigo Petacco, page 1573.

21 Second World War, The Pacific, David Horner, page 50.

22 Second World War, The Pacific, David Horner, page 50.

23 Leyte Gulf 1944: The World's Greatest Sea Battle, Bernard Ireland, page 9.

24 Leyte Gulf 1944: The World's Greatest Sea Battle, Bernard Ireland, page 22.

25 Leyte Gulf 1944: The World's Greatest Sea Battle, Bernard Ireland, page 47.

26 Strategy, BH Liddell Hart, page 335.

27 On-line interview with Alex Rovira in elpais.com, April 20 2005, Hitler's birthday, by the way.

28 Batallas decisivas del mundo occidental [Decisive Battles of the Second World War Decisive Battles of the Western World and their influence into History], (Volume III), JFC Fuller, page 695.

29 Second World War, The Pacific, David Horner, page 60.

30 United States Strategic Bombing Summary Report (Pacific War), US Secretary of War page 19.

31 Second World War, The Pacific, David Horner, page 56.

32 United States Strategic Bombing Summary Report (Pacific War), US Secretary of War page 10.

33 United States Strategic Bombing Summary Report (Pacific War), US Secretary of War page 10.

34 Second World War, The Pacific, David Horner, page 64.

35 Crónica militar y política de la Segunda Guerra Mundial [II World War], Arrigo Petacco, page 2273.

36 Crónica militar y política de la Segunda Guerra Mundial [II World War], Arrigo Petacco, page 2278.

37 Second World War, The Pacific, David Horner, page 64.

CHAPTER 11

1 Batallas decisivas del mundo occidental [Decisive Battles of the Second World War Decisive Battles of the Western World and their influence into History], (Volume III), JFC Fuller, page 266.

2 "Why good companies go bad", Financial Times, Donald N. Sull, October 3 2005.

3 "What is Strategy", Harvard Business Review, Michael Porter, November - December 1996.

CPSIA information can be obtained
at www.ICGtesting.com
Printed in the USA
LVHW102111290721
694063LV00011B/216